Thinking about being good

Published in the UK in 2023 by Mid Sussex Press

Paperback ISBN: 978-1-7394184-0-3
eBook ISBN: 978-1-7394184-1-0

Cover design and typeset by SpiffingCovers.com

Thinking about being good

A Memoir by

Penny Rome

For my girls – with endless love.

Prologue

It's September and the leaves are turning and I'm creating my fantastical worlds. I love seeing a world – my world, in miniature – a world where everything is topsy-turvy. This all started the other day when I found a beaten-up log. It had gouged out areas, deep grooves. I found it fascinating and took it home. It was rotten but I chose to ignore that, telling myself that a lick of varnish would do the job. I hit eBay, sending off for miniature goldfish and miniature grasses. I wanted to create a pond or lake and decided to make it with glycerine. But even though I think the wood has been waterproofed the glycerine disappears and my fish lie dead.

I buy miniature trees and miniature blackbirds, but the trees are too bushy and there is nowhere for them to go. The birds sit forlornly, still in their eBay packaging, and every day I'm reminded that I really would like to create a tree to sit my birds in. I've never been very good at drawing, however, which adds to my frustration. On my dog walks I look out for twigs or small branches that resemble a tree in miniature. Finally I have a collection.

Whenever I think of blackbirds, I start to sing my tuneless rendition of that old Beatles song, 'Blackbird'. *'Blackbird singing in the dead of night'*, but I only know the first line and even that brings tears to my eyes. Goodness knows why. I have a superstition about magpies, which must have started at school. What's required is that, upon seeing a magpie, you count backwards from 10 then say, 'Good morning, my Lord'. If you don't, you'll have bad luck. When a friend of mine sees a magpie, she whistles and waves her hand. You can imagine the muddle when we spot one while in the car together. I've never worked out when spotting a magpie in the afternoon if you have to say, 'Good afternoon, my Lord'.

I keep the log for ages with its dead fish and dried up stuck on autumn leaves but which are now all crinkly and disintegrating with a single touch. I'm always wondering what I should do with it until I decide to return it to the earth and put it back where I found it amongst the beetles, worms and woodlice that can make it their home.

Perhaps my strange thoughts go back to my days in India with my castles, kings and princesses all imagined under the water in our swimming pool.

These days such thoughts, such obsessions, manifest themselves in making lists, something that's become a habit, an addiction even. Now don't get me wrong, I like it. It started many years ago when my boss in my third job sat me down and said: "The best way to know what you're doing every day is to make a list. Call it an action list, and when you've accomplished a particular task on that list, cross it out. At the end of every day you start again and write a new list. Sometimes the list will be ridiculously long and other times, not so much. But it is a huge help to start to make this a habit in your life."

I began doing it then and I still do it now and *oh my goodness*, but it is a huge help. Making a daily list is enormously liberating. For starters, I have no worries about forgetting to do something because all I have to do is refer to my list. I have more than one list now. As well as a daily to-do list, I have a last-thing-at-night list, which reminds me of such things like my daughter is catching the 8.06 train instead of the 8.32 or that her friend is having a sleepover the following Tuesday and "Can I go, Mum?" I've realised that when information is given to me at 10pm I have switched off, so writing stuff down helps.

So, basically, I am a list person. I have my Christmas card list, my Christmas letter list (yawn), my diary (not written in every day but regularly enough) and my gratitude list, which includes my little pointers list. I reckon with all this *I* have become a habit or at least I inhabit a habit. My life has structure to it and there's rarely any drama. I'm never late to anything or in a rush to get anywhere. I'm usually awake at 5.30am and in bed by 10pm. I meditate every day but I don't beat myself up if I don't manage a whole 15minutes. Maybe 'routine' is the correct word. I like it, particularly the fact I don't take any worries to bed and that I can sleep peacefully. I ask myself, *Have I turned into my mother?* She was incredibly organised and efficient, which I like to think I am too. I have definitely got my mother's feet.

As for my looks, frankly there's not a marked difference to my ever-thinning lips. The corners dip south and I can't seem to make them into a smile again. Daily, I try to get rid of my top lip smoking wrinkles. Every day I s-t-r-e-t-c-h my top lip wide, pulling it down over my top teeth. It's no good.

I used to laugh a lot but lost that ease of giggles and laughter during my 17 years of marriage, much of it spent unhappy, frustrated and what I've now come to realise as fear. I'm sure the corners lifted up when I was young but ever since my miserable years, as I call them, the lips have sunk. It really isn't an attractive look. Sometimes I think I have a smile on my face but when I look in the car's rear-view mirror I find I don't have a smile at all, only a straight line – a grimace even. I lie in bed on my right side – my mother told me never to lie on the other side, the heart side, as it could give me a heart attack. Honestly, the things she came out with and I believed her! So I lie there on my right, my hand lifting my lip and cheek upwards hoping for the desired effect of a smile.

It's the same with my boobs. For some reason whenever I think about my breasts in general I hum, *'Swing high, swing low, sweet chariot'*. We used to laugh at my school friend, Susie, who used to be able to fling her boobs up to her shoulders to wash underneath. When we were teenagers, my best friend and I were delighted that not even a pencil could lodge under our pert and fulsome boobs. Sadly, these days, my best friend says she can get the whole of WHSmith under hers. I call my bras my 'Cross your heart living daylights bras'. There was a brand called Cross Your Heart by Playtex back in the day, but goodness knows why I have these strange ideas and choose such a weird name for my very ordinary bras.

All those times in London when I would pass workmen on my way to the office and they called out, "Cheer up, love, it might never happen!" I guess I must have looked glum. Not that I minded. With a wolf whistle and an ''Ello darlin'', I felt great. I knew that whatever this certain something was I could use it to my advantage. One example is when I'm getting a quote for some work that needs doing. Oh yes, I can become oh-so-charming and flirtatious and invariably get the work done for less. I like this – I like this a lot.

Today I'm content. Definitely some of this contentment is down to my beautiful black Labrador, Tolly. She brings me such joy even when I don't want to get up at flippin' five o'clock in the morning. We named her Tolly after the Tollygunge Club in Calcutta where I spent many happy times as a teenager drinking Thums Up – India's Coca-Cola equivalent (without the 'b'). Obviously, we couldn't call her Tollygunge. You can't call a gorgeous, shiny black Labrador a name with 'gunge' on the end of it. She's actually a duchess, don't you know, on her kennel club certificate.

So, my morning routine goes something like this: I hear the swish of Tolly's boomerang tail that she bangs on the bed in the hope I'm awake. Next, a heavy paw lands on my stomach. Then, a wet nose tries to lift my arm up.

"Come on, come on, come on," she goes.

"All right, all right," go I. And I turn over for the first of the day's doggie strokes except they have to be quick because she needs a wee and so do I. It's up and downstairs for a trip to the garden (*I* don't wee in the garden, I'm not like Sarah Francis in *Patrick*), kettle on and Tolly's breakfast. I make a huge mug of sliced ginger in hot water for me plus two krill oil pills, a turmeric pill and my pill for high bloody cholesterol. I've been on the statins for so long that my reading is down to a 2, so does that mean I'm cured, I wonder? Then we're back upstairs; Tolly for a snooze and me to read my book. Today it's Abigail Thomas' 'A Three Dog Life'.

I particularly love the very early mornings. I delight in getting up when it's just beginning to get light, especially in spring. Although the birds have been chattering away for a while, the world to me is still, silent and sleepy. A low mist moves slowly across Pheasant Field as Tolly and I meander through the peaceful woods. I see the white anemones, still sleeping, their heads bowed until they lift their pretty heads to greet the sunrise. I hear the woodpecker busy-busy-busy tap-tap-tapping. Everything is slowly waking. Sometimes I will quite suddenly spot a deer, rigid and absolutely still but ready for instant flight as Tolly uncaringly careers through the trees towards it. I see pairs of squirrels playing, chasing up, down and round and round trees. It is pure joy being out here as if I am the only human being alive. At these times I feel immensely alive and in harmony with my surroundings, so I give thanks out loud for this brand new day that I am fortunate to greet, saying, "Thank you for allowing me to walk on your good earth."

At other times, I plug myself in to either Radio 4's *Today* programme or listen to one of my many podcasts. Oooh, and I love *The Archers* omnibus. Somehow, though, Nick Robinson drives me nuts, especially when he says, "I need to hurry you up. We haven't much time..." Does he not realise he's just wasted time saying that? I turn off and decide that today I will walk and look – I mean *really* look – at what's around me. I want to absolutely notice. I want to enjoy the woods, which are silent except for Tolly who is bouncing and splashing in the streams, living in her moment and never blaming anyone with her waggy tail and gorgeous smiling face.

Of course, my life was not always like this...

Part One
Beginnings

In 1988, my friend Jane gave me a Winnie-the-Pooh diary. I didn't think much of it at the time, but by the time my daughter, H, turned two I had rediscovered it and began using it. I hoped that the writing would lighten my mood and thought that by writing everything down maybe I could get the angst, anger, fear and worry out of my head and onto the page. This created another habit. I've now been keeping diaries for over 30 years.

But my childhood came before my diary writing and this is what I recall…

Chapter One

The Early Years

I was born just after the days of the Raj. Well, nine years and seven months after, actually, in February 1956. My father was a tea planter and I lived with my parents on a tea plantation. I was a tea planter's daughter, an only child, and you could say I was a third generation Indian because my mother was born in India, as was her mother before her.

Being born so soon after India's independence, and being a child of the late 50s in India, the white British man and woman were still very much in charge. They were masters of all that they surveyed and, in the case of my mother, rulers of the roost.

My father was the assistant manager of the Rajmai Tea Estate in Jorhat, Assam, Northeast India. My birth was at the Christian Mission Hospital 40 miles away over a dirt track. It's very annoying, but I have no precise knowledge of what time I was born – I don't think I ever asked my mother although I have a vague memory of her saying I was born at 11pm. My father hadn't a clue. He wasn't at the hospital for my birth. Husbands weren't in those days.

It is a wonder how I came to be. My parents were not the lovey-dovey type and never ever showed affection to each other, certainly not in front of me. The atmosphere was very much one of 'One mustn't show one's feelings, one mustn't cry in public.' No emotion was to be revealed. Ever. It all comes down to that stupid British thing of the stiff upper lip. Everything was to do with appearances. We must all be the same; one mustn't rock the boat.

Like the Indian roads, life in those days was rough. There was no TV, no radio, British newspapers arrived several weeks late and there was no air-conditioning. In winter the temperatures could get as low as 10°C but it could be sunny and dry and therefore wonderful to feel cool and be able to walk about without dripping with sweat ('No darling, it's not sweat', my mother would say, 'we perspire'). But once March hits the temperatures soar to a sweltering 30°C or 35°C with added humidity. With the constant buzz of cicadas, everyone seems to move in slow motion and even cooling off in the swimming pool doesn't work, as the water is warm.

This was the time of India's fledgling independence. The one thing us British gifted India for her independence was bureaucracy – paperwork – mountains and mountains of the stuff, and then India doubled the bureaucracy and did the same with *its* paperwork.

My father went to India in 1949, two years after independence, on the advice of his Uncle George, a tea planter on the plains of Assam. When Uncle George came home on leave and regaled my father with stories of elephant rides, tiger hunts and camping in the jungle, I guess he thought that becoming a tea planter would suit him. And it did.

Uncle George had two wives. His real wife, the British one, had lived in England and stayed here for the education of their two boys, but while in India, Uncle George had a second wife, or more accurately, an Indian lady that he'd taken a fancy to. They produced six children so he must have fancied her a great deal – my father eventually employed all of them. I believe this sort of thing happened a lot. There was one tea planter I heard about who always carried a mattress in the back of his car in case he got lucky.

I try to imagine what my father's life would have been like in those early days when he was a young man starting out, having moved to a completely different country, cooped up in a small bungalow with that relentless heat. The moving is one thing but leaving your whole family and friends behind must have taken huge courage.

My father was the most junior of juniors, the white assistant to the white British manager of a tea plantation. I like to think of Assam as a county but since it's the size of England and Wales put together, it's more like a small country. And although the heat would have been exhausting, I know there were camps in the jungle because I too went on a couple of these in my younger years. There were fishing trips, elephant rides and, I'm sorry to say, tiger hunts for my father in his bachelor days. I have a photo of him with his foot on the belly of a dead tiger he'd shot. There were a couple of tiger skins on the floor as well as a leopard's skin that came with us in our various house moves. Camps were set up along the banks of the Borelli River and it was exciting riding in on an elephant with the tents surrounded by strings of tin cans to sound the alarm should a wild animal try to come in. Fires were lit as another deterrent as well as for cooking. Our house servants came with us.

All junior tea management men were white in those days. My father was a junior-nothing in a large British tea company called George Williamson & Co. This was his apprenticeship, which would last five years before he was permitted home on his first leave. He started this tea planter's life at 21 years old.

A couple of thousand miles away in Kotagiri, Ootacamund, my mother was caring for her own mother who had become unwell. I assume this as the only piece of written information I've got about my mother ends in 1947. Up until then she'd worked in various positions for the Women's Army Corps in New Delhi, followed by a transfer to Quetta, Pakistan. She was released from the Army in December 1947. I know nothing after that, but I like to think she went down to the hill station of Kotagiri in Ooty to be with her mother. That's where my grandparents had retired to and where my grandmother died in 1954. My grandfather had died in England a few years earlier – he was a lot older than his wife and in his late 50s when my mother was born.

My parents met on board a ship. My father was taking his first home leave and my mother had packed up what was left of the family home following her mother's death. She was 35 then and would have considered herself very much on the shelf. I expect she was feeling disappointed, maybe ashamed that she wasn't married, which is no doubt why she spent many years nagging me to find a husband. But it was serendipity that brought my parents together because they were utterly suited for the life they had when they returned to India as husband and wife after six months in England.

There was a story my father told about the early years when he and my mother were in India together. They once held a dinner party where guests were invited for 8pm. When no-one had arrived by 8.45pm, my father decided he'd had enough so he shut and locked the front doors, turned off all the lights and they went to bed. My parents were sticklers for punctuality and I have inherited this too. I will either be early or absolutely dead on time.

My father had a couple of pets, a monkey called Jimmy and his spaniel, Jill. Jimmy had a lady monkey friend and Daddy said he died of a broken heart when she was killed. My parents had been married less than two years when my mother became pregnant with me.

I don't really recall much interaction with my parents apart from the odd bedtime story of *Our Island Story: A Child's History of England* read to me by my mother. We didn't have neighbours as such. We were situated in a large compound garden and beyond this our servants had concrete rooms to live in and further afield were the houses that the other tea workers lived.

Gwennie came to my mother before I was born to look after her during her pregnancy and then to look after me. She was my ayah – or nanny – and stayed with us long after she was needed. It wasn't me that required looking after in the end since she remained with my parents even when I was schooled in England. I know of one family who so loved their ayah that they brought her to the UK. She was apparently happy to do this, leaving her own family and children behind but sending back money.

I loved my Gwennie. She was a tiny but ever-loving presence, always there and standing in the shadows. Every night she would put me to bed, singing sweetly and gently, '*Nini, Baba, Nini; roti, makan chini* (sleep, baby, sleep; bread, butter and sugar); *roti makan hogia, chota baba rogia* (bread butter finished, baby awake)'. I love bread, butter and sugar and still enjoy a slice even now.

Gwennie was a Khasi from the hill station of Shillong in the now Meghalaya district of Northeast India, near what is today the border with Bangladesh. Her Khasi uniform was a blouse and, over that, a loose sarong-type cloth held up by a knot on one shoulder. This was what all Khasi women wore.

Gwennie and I regularly had tea in her shed beside the cookhouse. It was just one windowless room and I can picture us now having hot, sweet, milky tea, sitting on our haunches (I wish I could still do that now – sit on my haunches, I mean). We had bread and butter for dipping into the sweet tea or sometimes it was warm toast and butter, which was much easier to dunk as it didn't disintegrate and fall into the cup. I loved beginning the hot humid days like this.

"This just will not do, Penny," was my mother's regular refrain as she swept down the stone path to find me – or more likely check on me to ensure I wasn't fraternising with the servants. My mother once told me, 'Oh dear, you're behaving like a native'. The thing is, I *was* a native. I already spoke fluent garden Hindi. The only difference was the colour of my skin – milky-white (burns easily) and rarely goes brown.

Then there was the trouble I had with leeches. I had to burn the damn things off my legs. You could never pull them off. They stuck to you like glue as they feasted on your blood. Disgusting. But pour some salt on them and they will melt off and die. I loved seeing them melt. You can burn them with a lit match too. Daddy did that to himself, but I wasn't allowed to use matches then. There was one time – I think I was about 11 – when I thought I'd got my period and my mother was so proud, coming into the bathroom and giving me a whole pep talk about how I was now a woman. She didn't go as far as explaining about boys and sex though – that would never do. But it was only a couple of spots of blood and it turned out a leech had somehow wormed its way to my groin. Ewwww!

Hill stations were towns founded by European colonial rulers around 3,000 feet upwards in the low mountains of India. Shillong was the one mostly favoured by those British workers in Assam so they could get away from the heat of the plains. It was a drive of more than four hours to get there, a pleasant journey as it got ever cooler as the car climbed up the gentle mountain slopes. It is a beautiful place and at least 10 degrees cooler than on the plains. We stayed at The Planters Club – now called The Shillong Club – designed for the British to enjoy the fresher cooler air and for children like me to… well, I'm not sure quite what. But I don't remember ever being bored.

***

Gwennie was my sanctuary, a safety net if you like. She was always there comforting me when I'd scream the place down when my parents went off, yet again, to the club for the evening. She never ever got cross, treating me with patience and constant kindness. My Boneys were another huge comfort. Boneys is a handkerchief with a frill all around the edge. The frill is critical. If the handkerchief doesn't have a frill, it's no good for what I need it for. I'd twist one corner of the frill into a point, which I licked. With my left thumb stuck in my mouth I'd dab the handkerchief so it became wet and cool and gently dab it onto the end of my nose. Such joy and pure comfort – I did need a lot of comfort then.

***

"Oh goodness, your hair, darling; what is to be done with it?"

I don't understand and haven't a clue what she's talking about.

"Well, darling, it's just so untidy and one can't go out to dinner looking like that."

My mother had stiff, permed hair. It was hairsprayed to within an inch of its life except there was no life left in it. She called it flyaway hair but there was no way that hair could have flown anywhere and no way could you run your fingers through it either. My mother was of a generation where running fingers anywhere on your body wasn't the done thing. So, what with her hairstyle and tri-weekly visits to the hairdresser for a comb-out, her hair was dead.

My youngest has really long hair, which doesn't quite reach her bottom, but when my mother was a lot younger her blonde hair did – reach her bottom, that is. Daddy said that's why her hair turned brown because she wiped her bottom with it.

***

At bedtime Gwennie would brush my hair 100 times then plait it or put it in bunches. When I last saw her in 1962, she cooked me the most delicious curry in her tiny concrete shack of a room. One corner was her bathing and washing-up area beside which was a small single stove. On the left side of this tiny room with its clay floor was her single rope bed. Gwennie also took me to visit her family's main house in Shillong, which was made of bamboo and built on stilts. A wide ladder approached the entrance and the whole of the front was open. It was really quite palatial and I loved our visits there though I often wondered how it would have stood up against a major rainstorm or strong winds. She was so proud of her son, Cyril, even though he'd basically stolen this house from her and left her in a tiny shack.

Gwennie always slept on the floor beside my bed when my parents went out, which as I said, they did a lot. I was scared of the dark and worried there was a monster under the bed. I'd pull the covers up over my head and leave a teeny-weeny gap for my nose. It was especially important that I couldn't see out, all those shadows and monsters, especially the ones under my bed who were ready to scratch my legs if I dared get out. Sometimes I would place my hands under the pillow so that my fingers could search for a cool spot, only for them to find a cockroach racing by.

My early memories are vague. I do recall a big playpen on an open veranda with toys. I remember a huge wooden doll's house and a rocking horse that swung to and fro. It wasn't one of those silly stuffed ones that, years later, was all I could afford for my youngest. Mine was on a stand with a long swishing tail. I called him Raja and together we'd magically gallop all over the world, which to me was only to the edge of the veranda. The only times I was allowed into my parents' bedroom and onto one of their beds was on Christmas morning – and that can't have been often as I think I only ever had three Christmas mornings with them. There were definitely no hugs as I climbed rather starchily and carefully onto my mother's bed and certainly no bouncing on the mattress. There was a distance between us and I always felt I needed to be on best behaviour. I do remember one occasion, however, when I opened my stocking to find one or two goodies in it including an orange, some chocolate and a few nuts. I gave a similar stocking to my oldest once thinking this was a family Christmas tradition to be followed. I guess she would have been about three and the look on her face when she got to the nuts and orange was priceless.

You'd think the fact that I was born in India would mean that some of that eastern philosophy – yoga, om, etc – would have rubbed off on me. It didn't. I speak Hindi fluently and I've got a whole load of Buddhas in various states of repose, but up until 1989 when my father retired and left India, I was completely bloody ignorant and I'm sorry about that. I wish I'd taken more notice but I was too busy growing up and feeling privileged in my Indian life of servants, chauffeurs and cooks taking care of my every need. I didn't bother looking around. I didn't ever have to make my bed, hang my clothes up or do the laundry – nothing. I didn't have to do a thing on the many holidays I had out there either. Instead I read books that my father discarded, my favourites being crime novels by James Hadley Chase and listening to LPs of musical theatre shows that my father loved – *Salad Days'* 'We're Looking for a Piano' and Richard Burton singing songs of *Camelot* such as 'If Ever I Would Leave You'.

So, basically, I was around six when my remembered life began. For the next couple of years all-sorts happened, but before that age nothing really did.

Chapter Two

Boarding School and Mountains

It was after midnight on an ordinary night on Borbeel Tea Estate. Well, that's not true, it probably wasn't midnight but it was definitely dark. My father was now the manager of this tea estate, the second plantation he'd moved to. By this time, I was used to the small tremors of Assam earthquakes and I was used to seeing the fireflies dancing in the black, velvet smooth night sky, appearing to intermingle with the distant stars. I was used to the cicadas' endless chirruping.

I had an interesting bedroom arrangement whereby my actual bed with bedside table was within a mosquito-proof wire mesh wooden frame. My room was huge but dark. Contained in this wooden frame was a door, which led out to what my childish eyes perceived as an enormous space with wardrobes covering the whole length of one wall. On the other side was a wall dividing my bedroom from my parents' bedroom. Their bedroom was light and spacious with windows all the way down the far wall, whereas my room was crowded with things – wardrobes mainly, and darkness. I recall there was only one window, which was never opened due to the need to keep the heat out and the cool in.

Then came a sudden BOOM! A large chunk of wall that divided my outer room from my parents' fell into my room. I woke with a start, befuddled, not understanding why my bed was moving around and why the floor was turning sideways. I cried silently. *Where are Mummy and Daddy? Why aren't they here? Will a monster come through the gaping wall?* I crept slowly out of bed. It was very dark and choke-inducing with smoke and debris in the air.

Suddenly I saw flashing lights coming down the corridor. Servants and Mummy and Daddy were rushing towards me. I was hysterical. "Mummeeeee!" I wailed. They spoke very calmly

"Oh darling, not to worry, it's just an earthquake."

"Mummy, please can I come and sleep in your room?"

"No, silly. Go back to bed. It was nothing; everything is fine."

And now my parents were laughing. *What on earth could possibly be so funny?* I hiccoughed madly, tears streaming down my face.

"Oh darling, can't you see that spider over there making funny faces at you?" asked my mother, trying to cheer me up.

Eeek. I HATE spiders. I'm sure my parents meant only to distract me, but I was terrified. I crept back to bed like the good girl I was and knew that as long as I had the covers over my head and couldn't see out then it stood to reason no-one could see me.

This is the only thing I remember from my father's days in Borbeel. At the age of five I was sent to boarding school 6,500 feet up a mountain in Darjeeling. All this was very normal in those days and it wasn't just me being sent away at such a tender age. There were – ooh, let me think – at least five of us from Assam, boys and girls, while others came from Darjeeling itself. Looking back, I think going to school at such a young age was a little too early. I was still wetting the bed – or perhaps I was wetting the bed because I was sent away. Plus it was very, very cold on this mountain.

My Darjeeling school, St Andrew's, was tiny. In my imaginings there might have been 200 children here, but in fact there were only 40, all of whom were white. To get all that way up from the plains of Assam took an entire night with the final part of the journey usually by pony. Mine was called Silver – he was big and white, but as I was only five everything was bigger than me. The school had huge, silver entrance gates, so big I imagined they led to heaven. There you go, head in the clouds already!

We were put on an overnight train from the Assam province capital Guwahati to Darjeeling's main station, Siliguri. Our parents took it in turns to accompany us on the journey, which took just over eight hours, providing a picnic supper of sandwiches, hard-boiled eggs and roast chicken. We'd sleep on bunk beds, heads at opposite ends and feet meeting in the middle. I'm not quite sure how we got from Siliguri station to Darjeeling central – it could have been on the now famous narrow-gauge railway or perhaps by bus. Our ponies would be there to meet us and, on one occasion, Silver decided not to follow the others and escaped down a side street. It was only through the goodness of a rather large man who stretched his arms out wide when he saw me, that Silver's escape was halted.

Since then I have been slightly scared of riding and have only managed to ride the most docile of ponies. My mother tried to get me to enjoy riding and took me to the army base camp where soldiers rode mules, but I never really took to it. My grandmother, Gaga, also did her best in trying to encourage my riding, but when the teacher put me on a pony so small my feet skimmed the ground, that was it – I didn't want to go riding anymore. I started to regain my confidence in horse riding when my best friend in the whole wide world, Jax, had a pony called Danny when I would have been 13 or 14.

My school had two dormitories – one for boys, the other obviously for girls. The beds were metal and I remember them being cold, but perhaps that was because of the bedwetting. I spent many cold, wet nights there and was always coughing, which I tried to disguise under the covers. In 1962 Darjeeling there was no central heating, no carpets and often jackals would wander around the corridors outside the dormitories at night. If you've never heard a jackal's cry, it's a really eerie sound and terrifying when you're lying in your cold bed in the dark at the age of six.

When any of the other tiny little children asked what my name was I'd say, 'Oh, it's Penelope Lorimer Rome' (much later discovering that Penelope means Weaver in Greek mythology, which is interesting as I try to weave this story). It took me quite a while to work out when asked my name that I didn't have to give it wholly, just Penny would do.

The arduous train journeys to and from home were only made for the three-month school holiday from December through to beginning of March. I do remember other breaks when my parents came up to Darjeeling and take me out for lunch or tea. They would stay at the Planters' Club, but I don't recall ever staying overnight with them on these visits. There were weekends when I'd stay with my friend Caroline, her parents and big sister, Judy, at Tukdah Tea Estate where her father was superintendent. Judy taught me how to ride a bicycle.

When us girls had a bath, which wasn't often, we were wrapped in towels beforehand and had to queue outside in the freezing cold before being allowed into the shed. While outside, if you looked up and over the top of the shed roof, the mountain view was staggering, but when you're little you don't take much notice of views. Inside, there were three tin baths surrounded by complicated pipework. It was two girls at a time in the lukewarm tub and six children using the same water. By the time the last pair got in the water was cold. I don't recall the boys having a bath at all.

There was no heating in the shed – no heating, full stop, as well as lukewarm water, metal beds, making the whole experience just very miserably cold. At six years old though, you don't think – you take whatever it is as it *is*. You're with grown-ups and I guess I assumed they knew what they were doing. But I do remember the mist, rain and snow on the distant mountains.

There was a choice of three playgrounds and a playroom at this school. The playroom had cupboards with doors and within each were shelves for sweets. The cupboards were low enough for us to climb up onto. Behind, there were curtained windows and also where Bobby Morris kissed me.

The bottom main playground was for roller skating and hair plaiting. The middle playground consisting of huge, magical-like silver gates was where we played kiss chase and cowboys and Indians – I was always an Indian.

The third and my favourite playground, which we were only allowed to play on at weekends, was all grassy green with masses of nooks and crannies for hide and seek. The danger here, though, was that it abutted the main mountain road with only a short ineffective fence. Often sinister-looking Buddhist monks in their long black robes would saunter past and spend time just looking. Our view was magnificent across the Himalayas to Kanchenjunga, but did I appreciate this? No, not at all.

My school days were abruptly interrupted when China invaded India in 1962. I was only little and really didn't understand why I, along with the four other children whose parents were tea planters in Assam, had to leave so suddenly in the early hours. I clambered sleepily into the car and began the two-day, 400-mile drive to Calcutta where my parents were to meet me. Before we left, I was presented with a book – *Heidi*.

I was told my mother was ill when we got to Calcutta and couldn't see me for a couple of days and that my father had remained at the tea garden. I'm not sure how he was going to fend off a Chinese invasion all by himself, but there we are. There is a photo of him lounging on a sofa with a drink in his hand, so I guess that was how it was done – sozzled.

I stayed with the family that had driven me down, waiting for my mother. Only many years later was I told the truth, by which time I was an adult. My mother, who at the outbreak of war decided the grand piano needed to be hidden in the swimming pool, didn't want to leave India and was furious that mothers and children were being forced to return to the UK. Summoning her attitude of 'Don't you know who I am?' she decided on a different course of action and put me in the Woodlands Nursing Home (at the time the main European hospital in Calcutta), to have my tonsils out. Well, why not? Coughs and colds were a regular occurrence for me, as well as earaches due to my penchant for spending a lot of time underwater playing in my make-believe worlds. Her plan worked perfectly.

I'd taken my favourite dressing gown with me – brown with a teddy bear sewn onto the pocket – the nurses said it sang songs. I also took my favourite Sally doll with the white hair, which made everyone laugh.

I was soon taken home to Assam and back to St Andrew's School when the war ended in November 1962 as China had declared a ceasefire.

Chapter Three

Phulbari Tea Estate, Assam

Assam is a beautiful province – miles and miles of paddy fields, all green and lush with giant storks and egrets walking delicately through. Buffalo and cows pull ploughs as women in saris with babies on their backs crouch in the water-filled rice fields planting the stalks. Older children run naked and laughing, pushing metal bicycle wheels with sticks.

In Assam, the tea gardens were split into South Bank and North Bank. When I was seven years old we left the South Bank where we'd experienced the earthquake and moved north to my favourite tea garden in the whole wide world – Phulbari. Our veranda overlooked the rice fields, a 3,000-plus acre patchwork of green and yellow shades stretching as far as my eyes could see. It was like a giant quilt with the rice swaying gently in the breeze, each block of rice field having narrow pathways separating each square. Outside our bungalow complex were rows of concrete houses with tin roofs for some of the 1,500 workers and their families. It was a sight to behold.

Phulbari means 'flower garden' and throughout the garden of our bungalow were masses of bougainvilleas. The bungalow had a thatch roof and that enormous front veranda with its tables and comfy soft cane armchairs. There was no front door and it's extraordinary to think now that the bungalow was open to everything and everyone and that only my parents' bedroom door and the door to the sitting room had locks. In the distance, there was a stone statue – I can vividly remember seeing a black widow spider sitting in its web strung between this statue and a nearby tree.

Most of my memories really start from Phulbari Tea Estate where my father had been promoted to superintendent, putting him in charge of three tea gardens in total. He was the boss at Phulbari itself, with two British managers working under him to help run the other two.

Early each morning, my parents had tea served in their room where they had a bed each. My mother actually drank lemon juice in hot water – so bitter that she would wince and make a sourpuss face. At night she'd always wait until the lights were turned off before removing her make-up, ensuring that my father never saw her make-up free. In the dark, she would then cover her face in Pond's cold cream and sometimes put the odd roller in her hair, even though she had her hair done three times a week, and then the crown of crowns, an elasticated plastic cap would be stretched over her head. She'd be up early to put her make-up on again before her tea was brought in.

Daddy's day would usually start at 6am with a visit to the tea factory. He would come home for breakfast (or hazri), before returning to the factory until tiffin time (a light lunch) at 12.30. Afterwards he'd have a siesta, a smoke and then consume the Indian version of Cadbury's chocolate. He would return to the factory at about 2.30pm or cycle around the tea gardens to deal with such problems as an elephant flattening an area – a regular occurrence. Tea, sandwiches and cake were served at 5pm sharp. Pink Gins at 6.00, Pink Gins at 6.30, pinch shins at 7.00, shrink I've had shnuff. Bed at 10pm.

The only part of the tea bush that is plucked are the two leaves at the top and the bud between them. These are still plucked by women, not machines, and you should see the speed they do it – it's a real skill. They are paid by the weight of the basket that they carry on their back, with the strap around their forehead. Among the tea bushes are tall trees with branches spread out to keep the heat of the sun off the bushes and workers.

Now that Daddy is a superintendent, his company car is a Jeep that enables him to go on inspections of the tea gardens. Our family car was a stupendous metallic blue Studebaker – really huge and American – not really suitable for the terrible roads. I loved to cycle and whizz round the veranda on my red bike. On Saturdays I would cycle out of our compound and perhaps visit the bazaar where there were masses of coloured glass bangles to buy. I desperately wanted one. At other times I cycled into the factory complex where the tea was cooked. The smell was intense and delicious. Even now I will occasionally catch a whiff of that pungent aroma of tea and it takes me straight back to that factory. The plucked tea was laid out on huge canvas beds or chungs, several stacks high. It was quite dark and cool in there, with an air of calm out of the sun. It was often deserted while the workers were having lunch or siesta and I found it spooky. I'd climb up the side of the chungs, being careful not to touch the canvases so thin they could easily break. I would hide in amongst them and play make-believe.

At other times of the day I would pop in to see Daddy in his office. He always had time for me and I was fascinated by his clerk – or babu – in the office next door who had filed his forefinger nail into the shape of a fountain pen nib, which he dipped into the inkwell to write with. I couldn't stop staring at him.

Our bungalow was on a small hill. In the distance to the right was the Harchurah Tea Estate, which the Telfers managed. To the left was a long, straight tarmac road along which convoys of huge army trucks would regularly lumber by. On our immediate left, on another small hill, was where Dr Oswald lived. He was really old and came over to give us our cholera, typhoid and goodness-knows-what-else injections. There was the one occasion when it was my turn for the dreaded jab and the needle went right through my arm and out the other side. I don't think Dr Oswald even noticed. Maybe it's that memory that means I never look when I have injections or am giving blood.

My father had boils on his bottom, though this was spoken of in very hushed tones, and there were all sorts of goings-on with jars, matches and Dr Oswald visiting. Today when I look up the meaning of boils in Louise L Hay's *Heal Your Body A–Z* book, which has become a bit of a health bible for me, it says they indicate 'Anger. Boiling over. Seething', which doesn't make sense because I only ever saw my father cross a few times. The first was when I went to plug something in with wet hands and he slapped me hard on my bottom with his leather slipper, and he did get extremely cross when I saw the films *The Devils* and *The Music Lovers* as a teenager when I was in Brighton with Jax. He expressed his anger by airmail letter, which was pretty much the only time he wrote to me. Another time, when I was about 14, he got cross because I called him 'Dad'. Everyone at school called their father Dad and I wanted to do the same since 'Daddy' sounded too babyish. 'Never call me Dad again', he had said. There was actually a fourth time, which I have outlined a bit later on.

Often my parents would have friends over for drinks and they would bring their children over to play. There'd often be a large crowd of us children playing together.

In the ginormous garden there were three very high palm trees, which could be seen from miles around and ensured I never got lost. Behind the bungalow was a wire chicken coop in which lived two hens, Pertilot and Chaunticlear, and a couple of pigs, Simon and Sally. Rosie the cow was kept in a pen two tennis courts away over by the swimming pool. I got pretty upset and cried when we ate the hens for our Christmas lunch, but my parents just laughed.

The pigs were my mother's idea. She wanted to breed them but after several months when nothing was happening on the baby front she asked my Uncle John what to do. He wasn't my real uncle, but in those days it was a mark of respect to call someone who was a friend of the family 'uncle'. He was the company's tea taster and not a pig breeder and his advice was to put some honey on Sally's rear to attract the male. Success would be inevitable, he said, but all hell broke out with all-sorts attracted to poor Sally's rear, mainly wasps and ants. It turned out both pigs were female!

On the back veranda, Mummy had two mynah birds that were supposed to be able to talk but never did. Daddy had to get his rifle out one afternoon because a python, or perhaps it was a cobra, had settled in the roof beams of the garage. The gardeners hung the dead snake from a pole and paraded it in front of us. I reckon the skin could have been made into a handbag for my mother because she did have a snakeskin handbag as well as a folded up, dried-up snakeskin when I went to clear up her things after she'd died.

The bungalow also consisted of a sitting room, the dining room and through that was the pantry. We had an all-round veranda. To the left stood my parents' room and two en-suite guest bedrooms. One of these rooms had air-conditioning but the rest of the house relied on ceiling fans.

All the guests that came out to stay, and there were many of them, stayed in the coolest guest room. Uncle John Trinick was our most regular guest. He spent a lot of his working life travelling the world visiting tea gardens. He was a highly regarded tea taster and was enormously respected. The Magors – the Magor of the company name McNeil and Magor – were honoured guests and everyone would run around making sure their stay was successful.

The walls were cream coloured and the windows had thick curtains to keep out the heat. The floors were red stone and cool to the touch, delicious in all that heat. I always remember my parents' bedroom being a mess, but I don't know why because my father was as neat as a pin. The fourth time I got told off happened after I'd borrowed his nail clippers but didn't put them back in the *exact* position where I'd found them. He was very particular.

Through my parents' bedroom was my small bedroom, which was really a dressing room divided from my parents' with a curtain, and then through my room was a bathroom where our black Labrador, Ringo, had her 13 puppies.

Every night without fail, the bearers – or house servants – would get our bedrooms mosquito-free by pumping a Flit gun filled with an insecticide spray called FLIT to kill off flies and mosquitoes because we didn't sleep under mosquito nets.

It was at night that everything came alive. Fireflies would shine their lights and the never-ending buzz of the cicadas made your senses alert to every sound. The most beautiful flower in the world, the Brahma Kamal named after the Hindu God of Creation, blooms for only one night every year. It stays in full bloom for just six hours then wilts in the morning, and it's believed that if you see it in bloom Brahma blesses you. It gives off the most gorgeous smell.

A highlight of a weekend was a Sunday boating trip down the Borelli River, a tributary of the mighty Brahmaputra. Boating sounds rather tame; it was more like gentle white-water rafting. Just as in England where we have the Sunday roast tradition, the Sunday tradition in my Assam days was the river fishing trip – another great family day out. My parents and I, along with other tea planters, wives, children, some servants and drivers, with Jeeps packed up with dinghies, fishing rods and picnics, would set off early. It was a riot, a fantastic day out with the great dinghy convoy negotiating the rapids, some people fishing, others jumping out to swim when we would stop for a break at Sonai Mook, a tiny sandy island with no trees.

There would be the Olivers with their boys Nigel and Rupert and daughter Hilary, the Telfers with their three children, the Graves with theirs, the Rosses, the Eastments – in other words, a big crowd. Nigel was really good-looking and Rupert was geeky and awkward, but he had a really strong backstroke. My favourite is front crawl.

My parents would be in separate boats. My mother was a serious fisherwoman, very competitive and at one point she was the North India champion. My father fished too and I rode with him in a second boat. There was that time when Mummy went sailing past and couldn't get back to Sonai Mook. She was way over the other side of the wide river and had the picnic with her, leaving Daddy and I with one banana to share. It was funny. The river had a strong current, so you had to be very careful not to drift. Although we helped with the rowing, each dinghy had a couple of boat boys. Our drivers stayed with the Jeeps, which were then driven down to the landing site at Potters Alley, which we got to in the early evening.

It was always tricky to reach the landing site. There was a large whirlpool that made our entrance extremely treacherous. The trick was to float ever so carefully on the far side of the river from the whirlpool and glide past it, then row like crazy, back-tracking upriver against the current to arrive at the landing post. It was exhausting and exhilarating at the same time. 'Maraga-maraga-maraga' (hit-hit-hit) the boat boys would shout as oars crashed into the water. I loved this. It was usually dusk when we arrived to find bonfires burning with pots of hot, sweet tea all ready for us.

Another weekday, just the mothers and children went on this trip. All the children stripped and rushed off for a cooling swim but not me since my mother insisted I wore an ugly swimming cap. I hated it. I was also made to wear a t-shirt over my swimming costume to stop me getting burnt – a good idea because only a few weeks earlier I'd returned from a day at the river in serious pain with a deeply discoloured back. You'll remember earlier I said I was white-skinned. It was crazily sore and not even possible to lie down in bed. My back turned into a landscape of large, white-domed blisters and my mother doused my bed with flour to soften the coarse cotton sheet. When was sun tan lotion invented? I don't remember ever using it.

That weekday that the mothers and children went to the river, I slipped on the steep clay bank and fell in the water and, before I knew what was happening, I was slowly pulled towards the whirlpool. Suddenly, Durjo, our driver, was crashing into the water and pulling me out. All I could hear was my mother screaming from the bank. I had no idea I was in any danger at all and was a bit embarrassed. I was soon in the water again.

Chapter Four

Meanderings and Musings

Our head bearer – or head servant – had two bearers under him. Then there was the cook (bobbachee) who had a pani wallah (washer upper) under him. The pani wallah would also report to the head bearer and take instruction from him. Malis (pronounced 'marlees') were the gardeners. My ayah, Gwennie, was staff of course, and then we come to the sweeper (jamadar). The poor man, he was the lowest of the low, and I'm talking here of his low caste. And don't ask me about where the night watchman or chowkidah came in. The caste system in India is seriously complicated. I guess only us Westerners find it so, or maybe just me. The hierarchy within the servant household had to follow the caste system rules.

The bearers wore smart, white-starched uniforms with splendid white turbans. Attached to the front of the turban was a brass badge with my father's initials. Pugli was our head bearer, which I thought was a strange name because 'pugla' means mad and he wasn't. Often the durzi (dressmaker) would arrive and plant himself on the side veranda to mend anything that needed mending. If I was there for the holidays, Mummy might ask him to copy a dress from one of her magazines for me. There wasn't much choice of materials where we lived as it was so rural, so whenever we were in Calcutta we would buy stuff at the New Market, which wasn't really new at all.

The malis spent pretty much all day mowing the lawns using a push-me-pull-you lawn mower. There was just so much lawn to mow, plus the two grass tennis courts. One mali was at the front of the machine pulling the long rope attached to the mower, with the other holding onto the handles at the rear and pushing. The malis and the sweeper wore dhotis, as did the cook. These look rather like a loose-fitting nappy for grown-ups – Gandhi wore one.

You wouldn't get our head bearer passing the time of day with the floor sweeper. Oh no. But this head bearer would chat to the cook and vice versa. The cook wouldn't talk to the floor sweeper either. What a lonely life the sweeper had.

Every morning without fail the head bearer would come to the breakfast table and take instructions for his tasks for the day ahead from my mother. The cook followed a short while later to take down the day's menu requirements. He then went off to market to buy the necessary ingredients with some money my mother gave him. There was a large store cupboard – or godown – filled with tins of this and that, various foods just in case. Scary krait snakes lived up in the wooden eaves. I'd only go in there if my mother was going in too.

I loved sitting out on the narrow back veranda directly outside the utility area from which the bearers served the food, convenient since it was right next door to the dining room. The kitchen itself was an outhouse down a concrete path. This building backed onto our boundary fence. Over that fence was barren land where sometimes an elephant would arrive with his mahout – or rider – sitting with his feet behind the elephant's ears hoping for some bakshish – a tip – just for making an appearance. My parents always did, as an elephant turning up was quite exciting, but I was a bit blasé – I suppose I always felt privileged.

In those days there was no such thing as a washing machine. What I mean is that, in all the time my parents were in India we never did have a washing machine. We had the dhobi (washing person) instead. He would visit twice a week and collect all our dirty laundry to take back to his hut, which was built nearby beside a large pond. The dirty clothes would be put in piles in my parents' bedroom with Mummy's knickers here and Daddy's pants over there. Then the counting would begin –1, 2, 3, ek, doh, teen, char, panch, chay, sart, art, noh, dus – and as he picked up each item of clothing, whatever it was would be flicked or snapped in the air and dropped into a pile. Once everything was counted and written in the dhobi book, the clothes would be wrapped in a large cotton cloth and flung over the dhobi's shoulder to be taken away. I was always impressed at how clean and white everything was when it was returned a couple of days later, the bright white sheets and Daddy's shirts all pristine and neatly folded. How was this managed when the dhobi lived in a simple concrete hut beside an unclean pond? I would hear the sheets and clothes being slapped, like a good steak, against a stone slab beating out the dirt – that much was obvious. The water where the clothes were rinsed was filthy and everyone including dogs and cows used the water pump.

At the side of the bungalow was where Ringo, my soppy, big, black, leggy Labrador slept and from where I'd throw balls for her and play hide and seek. Ringo was the first pet I really remember and was considered mine even though I was hardly there as I was away at school. As she got older she didn't want to play so much and Daddy brought home a puppy, which we called Loppy. She was a black lab too and all bouncy, which didn't please Ringo at all. Then came the day when there was something definitely not right with Ringo. She was foaming at the mouth and her eyes were going funny. I felt bad for spending so much time playing with Loppy and really not taking any notice of Ringo and thought that maybe that was why she was ill. I sat on the floor with her head in my lap, stroking her ears and saying 'Sorry I haven't looked after you properly. Sorry, sorry, and I promise I won't do that ever again if you'll just get better'.

But Mummy said gently that Ringo probably wouldn't survive the day. I cried and cried and then she was gone. I felt so ashamed. Such a good dog and all those 13 puppies she had. Mummy and I had to help feed them because Ringo didn't have enough nipples. When I look at my Tolly girl now, I wonder if perhaps she's a reincarnated Ringo or even Loppy.

Just beyond the main gate to our bungalow where our servants lived with their families was a row of small concrete huts. Those dastardly jackals roamed at night and if you heard a jackal bark seven times the cook said a child would die. Wild dogs called pie dogs – they are an actual breed called the Indian pariah dog but more commonly called Pie, Pye or Pi dogs – roamed around scavenging in packs and would add to the barking noise.

The servants' children and adults too would scrape up cow poo and shape it in their hands to make it flat. This would then be flung against their hut to dry in the sun and used for making a fire later.

Much to my mother's horror, I spent many happy times chatting with the servants. I felt truly cherished and perfectly comfortable in their company. They gave me sweet treats and treated me as one of their own. I was astonished at their kindness and how they could work in their thick cotton uniforms and turbans in all the heat. My mother didn't like me getting too close to them. I was terribly embarrassed by her attitude, which was really quite racist, and even though I didn't understand the meaning of the word 'racist' I guess I felt something akin to shame. My cheeks redden at the memory. 'Come now, Penny darling, that's enough chatting', she'd say. 'You must go and wash your hands'. For some reason, she always presumed our servants were dirty.

All the servants called me Baba, which was just so babyish and I didn't like it. Daddy was Burra Sahib (Big Man) and Mummy, Memsahib (I guess that means Mrs Man). I looked forward to the day they called me Missahib.

***

Life in 1960s Assam was very busy socially as long as you enjoyed playing tennis, squash, golf, swimming and, of course, drinking gin and whisky. If we weren't going down the river at the weekend then we'd go to the club. TV hadn't arrived yet and we barely had a telephone. In order to get hold of another number, one had to put one's finger in the relevant hole on the dial and hold the dial down once turned. One then had to shout down the phone and enunciate each word, so as an example, if you were giving out a telephone number it would go: 'Te*nnn*' with the emphasis on the 'n' so it sounded like 'Tenna'. And you had to raise your voice while talking extremely slowly and often you wouldn't get through at all.

Our club in Phulbari days was the Thakabari Club, almost an hour's drive away. Quite often in the monsoon season (the summer months, which were my school holiday), roads were impassable or the rickety wooden bridges would break. Our driver would have to detour and our journey would be even longer.

The club had a golf course, swimming pool, grass tennis courts galore, a clubhouse with bar and later, a squash court. Also present was a dance area and a stage, plus a screen for the showing of movies. The first film I ever saw was *My Fair Lady*, which was magical. There was lots of social drinking because, unless you were happy in your own company, happy to stay at home reading the week-old newspaper, club life was important. It wasn't open every day though, just Wednesdays, Saturdays and Sundays. Gwennie would come too to keep an eye on me while Daddy played golf and Mummy tennis.

My parents were very much part of the club social scene. Daddy was mad about films and theatre and, before I was born, he and Mummy would stage musicals with my mother playing the piano. She was a very good pianist. Daddy would rewrite the lyrics turning songs like 'Three Little Maids from School Are We' into 'Three Little Maids from Tea Are We'. There were also bridge evenings because both my parents loved the game.

When my parents went home on leave to England my father and I went to lots of theatre shows and films. I remember going to see *Bambi* when I must have been about 12. As soon as Bambi's mother was killed I started to cry and Daddy had to take me out – he was quite cross about it. Occasionally, it would be a theatre matinee followed by possibly two films at the cinema. It was very exciting if the new James Bond movie had come out. My mother would window-shop but buy nothing. My parents were really hard up money-wise as my father's salary was paltry. I only found out about this much later – our servants, flight costs back and forth to the UK and my education, etc – were all paid for by the tea company, so the impression was given that we were rich – certainly I felt that.

My father was an imposing man at six feet four inches. When he walked into a room everyone turned to look at him. He towered over everyone, a mighty bear of a man. He commanded respect. He also smoked from first thing in the morning, which is to say that a cigarette was the first thing he reached for when he woke up at 5am. He smoked whenever and wherever he could, which was pretty much all the time although I don't remember him ever smelling of smoke. He also ate sweets, which he would enjoy on his afternoon naps. He was stick thin, but he made me feel safe.

An extract from Calcutta's then daily paper, the *Dainik Basumati*, dated 6th December 1980 at a reception:

'Prince Charles met a British gentleman about seven feet in height. This middle-aged gentleman is Michael Rome. He is in India for a long time. After passing about 15 years in Assam he is now in

Calcutta. Mr Rome by the by said that he knew Assam as his own fingers. However, the number of Englishmen in Assam has now been reduced from one thousand to only five. Same is the condition in Calcutta too. The Prince became eager. He enquired "Why? Is there any legal bar for Englishman to remain in Calcutta? Those who have left this country have they done it voluntarily or was there any obstacles?" Mr Rome informed that there was no legal bar, but those who have left this country wanted environment of their likings. Moreover, during last few years many British industries changed hands.'

The first piece of jewellery my father ever bought me was a gold ring intricately set with an amethyst stone. Amethyst is my birthstone, but this wouldn't have been something my father gave any thought to. Another time I received an enormous smoky topaz ring set in silver when my father's racehorse, Royal Bear, won at the races. The ring was so big that it actually pulled my fourth finger down. These were the years when my father bought racehorses or, rather, he'd buy a leg or perhaps two legs, sharing the horse with his best friend Pearson Surita. Pearson was quite a character in Calcutta circles. He resembled a bloodhound dog, all jowly and sad-looking. I used to love visiting his bohemian flat in an ancient days-of-the-Raj house with his moth-eaten rugs, crumpled suits and bow ties. He was a cricket commentator and his grave is not far from my mother's in Bhowanipore Cemetery, so I'm glad he's keeping her company. He was a hoot. A visit to the races was a highlight of the Royal Calcutta Turf Club calendar and my parents had a box. The only time I saw Royal Bear race, she was knocked into the inside fence and, horror of horrors, had to be shot.

Daddy had a couple of nicknames for me, Penny Two-Shoes and Tuppence Ha'penny. From Mummy it was Penny Darling but always Penelope if she was cross. My close friends call me Penskew or Pen.

Chapter Five

Boarding School in England

"One more day of school, one more day of sorrow,
one more day of this old dump and we'll be home tomorrow.

No more spiders in the bath trying hard to make me laugh,
no more flies in my tea making googly eyes at me."

I am eight years old when I begin my boarding school life in England at PNEU Burgess Hill in Sussex. And that was the song we would sing on the last day of term. Our school motto was: I am, I can, I ought, I will. I changed that to: I'm not, I can't, I shan't and I won't.

PNEU as it was, now Burgess Hill Girls, is a girls-only day and boarding school. In my day there were more boarders than daygirls and boarders felt more superior to the mere daygirls. I joined in the second term of the school year and, believe me, this was not a good idea. Unknowingly, I did exactly the same with my oldest, which is probably why she struggled at first to make friends. When you join in the second term, friendships have already been made and my first term was horrible.

It's my birthday term and I'm going to be nine. Nobody speaks to me, which is really hard to cope with, especially as we share baths and are in dormitories of six. A few of the unpleasant things I experienced and of which were the norm are apple dumplings, when the sheets are turned inside out with cold and wet flannels placed inside your bed making it a mess. With this all going on, I felt homesick and spent many nights crying with my Boneys under the covers with just my nose sticking out, sucking my thumb. Boneys is never to be washed and becomes dirty grey in consequence, but it made me feel secure – my security blanket, my comfort.

So as I said, it's my birthday and the loose rule is that we open our birthday presents in front of everyone at the boarding house. Oakdene is my first boarding house for little girls of eight and nine years old and my friend Caroline is also here. We were at the same boarding school in Darjeeling because her father is also a tea planter. So, all my presents were laid out on the refectory table. There weren't many; it was the sheer size of two of them that caused trouble. The first big present was an enormous book called *The Fairy Princess* full of exquisite drawings. This was from my mother. The second was a tea chest, filled to the brim with Smarties (God knows how my parents got that organised) and, quick as a flash, was grabbed at by little girls all greedy for the sweets. Smarties everywhere. As for my beautiful book, this was later stolen and the pages all torn – I don't know to this day what happened to that book. This was the start of school life. It was horrid.

I was caught bouncing on my bed and Miss Hill the housemistress came and smacked me with a hairbrush very hard on my bare bottom, which was so unexpected I wet myself. Miss Hill, or Hilly to us, had a cold bath every single morning, which she would announce proudly and which probably accounted for her deeply purple nose and veined cheeks. She also decided that my hair needed cutting and would cut it randomly. From that incident my hair has become like straw – that's what I'm telling myself, anyway. She wouldn't be allowed to do that today.

At 10 years old we moved to Avondale, another boarding house run by Miss Duncan – or Dunk. She was very small in stature and walked with a stick because she'd had polio when she was young. Whenever it was half term or a school holiday, Dunk would say, 'I'm going off to my stately home'. It was years before we found out that her 'stately home' was actually a caravan.

Avondale was the middle house we lived in before moving up to the senior houses at school, which in those days were Silverdale East and Silverdale West. In actual fact they are one large Victorian building split in two. Jax is a daygirl but by this time has become a weekly boarder because her mother is sick. Her father died the year before and we like to think that her mum is dying of a broken heart. When her mother died, Jax became a full-time boarder and I guess we were drawn to each other because my parents were far away and her parents were no more.

***

We, that is, us four grandchildren, call my paternal grandmother Gaga, whom I mentioned earlier. She is my father's mother and becomes my legal guardian while I am at school and it is to hers that I spend most of my school holidays. Her eldest son, Peter, is married to my Auntie Alison and they have three girls. I wouldn't say that we were a very close family. Physical distance was one element of this with my father in India and Uncle Peter in Beirut and then Hong Kong and later to deepest, darkest Wales. Unfortunately, the only other person to stay near my grandmother and therefore near me was my father's younger sister, Biddy. Her real name is Daphne and I don't know why she's called Biddy. Although she lived and worked in London, she invariably returned to Gaga's house at weekends.

Biddy never really had anything nice to say, it was a constant moan: 'No, I can't bear to watch *the Morecambe & Wise Show* on TV', Biddy would complain. But Gaga and I loved it and watched with glee.

Up until the age of 14, every school holiday (apart from the summer break) was spent at my grandmother's large farmhouse. The house had been split into two, with one half being a bed and breakfast. However, when my grandmother bought it for the princely sum of £5,000, she returned it to one house and brought her mother, my Great Granny, to live in a granny flat up the second staircase. It was a grand house with a grandfather clock under the minstrel gallery, which formed part of the large dining room, home to a huge open fireplace and had a mantelpiece nobody could reach.

Great Granny was stone deaf and wore hearing aids that did little to improve the situation. Nonetheless, she always knew when I entered her room. I tried to do this silently as I was full of amazement that she was so completely deaf but could still 'feel' me entering her room. But it never worked. Great Granny farted a lot and played endless games of Patience and Gaga was rotten to her even though I suspect it was Great Granny's money that paid for the house and continued to support my spendthrift grandmother – all those bottles of gin for starters. Great Granny's hair was white with tight curls and she was one of 13 children. Her side of the family was called Martin.

It was my grandmother Gaga who married into the Rome family who hailed from Liverpool – Liverpool docks where my great-great grandfather was chairman. Gaga's father killed himself. He went up into the attic on the pretext of cleaning his guns and bang! Dead.

The house is on the outskirts of a village called Findon, right on the present A24, not far from Worthing town and next to Worthing Crematorium where Great Granny, Gaga and my father were cremated. Their plots are under a huge chestnut tree. There was no central heating in this house and in the cold winter months I spent many a joyful time sitting on the window seat in my bedroom, which, lucky me, looked out over the A24 dual carriageway. I would pick at the ice that had formed on the window pane. My bedroom had two walk-in cupboards. There was a third floor with its staircase behind a closed off door that led to the attic. The attic was a scary place and often I'd hear mice scrabbling about, although when Gaga said they were having tea parties it made me feel much better. Added to this, her dogs would suddenly bark for no reason, so I'd hide behind the sofa, you know – just in case.

In the garden there was an apple orchard with a hen house and one of my jobs was to collect the eggs from under the hens. I really didn't like sliding my hand under their warm bodies and spindly legs and got scared in case they pecked me. In another part of the garden, Gaga had Sally the goat that regularly tried to ram me with her horns. I was really scared of the geese that just hissed and attacked with their snake-shaped necks down low.

My grandmother was not all sweetness and light. Being so young, I didn't understand why Gaga was so cross all the time over really silly little things: 'Could you get me that duster from the cupboard under the stairs?' she might ask me, but when I picked one – and there were quite a few to choose from – she would say, 'No, no, not that one, you silly girl!' Everything was said in a crosspatchy way and she always had a wine glass above the sink with clear liquid in it, which I thought was water. I remember goodnight kisses and… what was that strange smell?

It's only relatively recently that I've realised my grandmother was a functioning alcoholic. Neat gin with perhaps a soupçon of water. Oh dear, all that driving around and driving me to school –

no seat belts in cars at that time. She was a fabulous cook though, even with her constant smoking. It was always Player's No 6 – the cheapest – lighting one cigarette from the butt of another. The thing is, you never quite knew if it was pepper sprinkled on top of the mashed potatoes or flyaway ash.

I realised that I inhabited two very different worlds. There was Gaga's house where I had to do chores like the washing-up, but then I went home to my parents in India where I didn't have to lift a finger to do anything. Where was home exactly?

Gaga grew up in Liverpool, moving to Anglesey in Wales after her marriage broke down and after giving birth to her three children. Her husband became an army captain in WWI, went off to war and returned asking for a divorce because he wanted to marry the nurse who'd cared for him when he got wounded. This was a scandal at the time, but my grandmother was not totally innocent. She became an army truck driver on the American base, which is where she learnt to drive. I am told there were many affairs, lodgers and 'guests' who stayed over.

I think I loved my grandmother, but she was so stern and mostly angry like her bloody geese and she threw out all my cuddly toys when she moved. She died aged 76 from lung cancer, not surprisingly. I was 19 and visited her a couple of weeks before she died. My father, knowing that she didn't have long, had flown over so we could visit her together. You might think that she'd be this wizened cancer-ridden old woman. Not a bit of it. She's still a crosspatch with me and when I had no choice but to serve up salad instead of the planned roast lamb because her oven and hob were broken, well! I think it was bitterness, too. That didn't help.

Chapter Six

Holidays

I'm on my summer holidays from school. Two months off, yippee! Unusually I'm not flying to India because Mummy and Daddy have flown home to England instead. It's funny how they always called England home. Daddy is on his three-month leave, which takes place every other year, but soon that will change to six weeks every year. All flights paid for by the tea company.

Mummy arrives first 'to get things ready for Daddy' whatever this means since there's nothing to get ready as they both stay at Gaga's, which is already ready, if you see what I mean. This year we're having a two-week holiday in Trearddur Bay, Anglesey, and will join my father's brother Peter, his wife Alison and their three daughters, my cousins – Gilly Mary is the eldest, followed by Jenny and Susie.

They've rented a large, furnished house set into a hill from which we can walk to the beach every day. Mummy and Auntie Alison will share the cooking, taking it in turns. The only trouble with this arrangement is that my mother cannot cook. I'm dead serious. Not even an egg. And since she was at boarding school and went back and forth to India, she's never really needed to learn. She can do a bowl of Corn Flakes or Puffed Wheat (Daddy's favourite), and she can make sandwiches. But as for anything requiring a cooker or frying pan? You can forget it.

Having never had to prepare or produce a cooked meal at any point in her life is possibly the reason why she has ideas of grandeur for my future and I. You can imagine her delight when she finds ready-made frozen fish fingers. Fantastic! Supper that evening was nevertheless interesting. Fish Fingers, still frozen, placed on the plate (my best friend Jax once tried to Sellotape a cracked egg together).

I can only imagine what my mother's young life was like because she never told me and I never asked. I reckon it was similar to the one I lived, except her mother would have spent more time in England because transport would have been so slow back then. There's a house in Burgess Hill that no longer exists that was substantial, as well as property in Kotagiri in Ootacamund. My mother's upbringing was very much days of the Raj. It's no wonder she was the way she was. I would think it must have been difficult for her to come to England for all those leaves that my parents took. I think she would have preferred to stay put carrying on with her 'good works'.

Staying with my grandmother Gaga can't have been easy either for my mother and I am sure she was treated very much as a guest, a visitor – someone they barely knew. Of course, they didn't know her well at all and she wasn't really treated as a member of the family. She would not have been included in general family chit-chat and gossip, everyone tiptoeing around each other with my poor mother not really understanding what her role was. Was she meant to try her hand at cooking? Could my grandmother, a fantastic cook, teach her? No, of course not.

Packing up my trunk for my return to school was something she'd never had to do. She had servants to pack for her and for me when necessary. Was she supposed to iron my school clothes? I'm sure my grandmother would not have stepped up to advise and help. My grandmother made my mother's life difficult, but once my father arrived, all this would change and Gaga would be all sweetness.

My Auntie Biddy is a difficult woman who thinks that going to church on a Sunday means a definite pass to heaven and that she can therefore be as nasty as she likes the rest of the week. When my mother came home in the early days for those trips, I can imagine how Biddy would have been on the sidelines; whispering loudly, sniggering and giggling at my mother's apparent incompetence. Biddy had visited Assam when I was a baby and there's a photo of her pushing me in a pram. Daddy said later that she was a total nightmare on that visit with endless complaining about the food – she didn't like curry! But when she started to have an affair with a married tea planter whose wife was away with the children in England, all hell broke loose and my father made her leave. She never returned nor was she invited.

***

I am 11 years old and standing with my grandmother, Gaga, at Heathrow Airport about to catch my plane to India for my summer holidays from boarding school in England. Yippee! Gaga is wearing her usual garb of tatty grey cardigan over a brown shirt of some sort and a knee-length tweedy skirt, which has been patched in places. Under the skirt she wears the most extraordinarily bright-coloured stockings. Today they are flaming orange and held up precariously with suspenders, the catch of which are stretched down and clipped to the stocking top just above the knees. This is not necessarily a problem until she sits down when her knees drop out to the sides and all is revealed as my cheeks start to burn and I want to die.

This is the first time I will have seen my parents since I was nine, but lucky me, from now on I'm going to see Mummy and Daddy pretty much every holiday, which is better than being with my grandmother. They manage this by trading in the first-class tickets that the company buys them for economy seats, which means they can pay for my flights.

Mummy says that with all this travelling I'll be really good at geography, but I don't understand how that could be when all I'm doing is travelling back and forth to Calcutta with the odd stop-off at Tehran or Rome.

It's not only the intense heat that smacks you in the face as you step off your BOAC plane at DumDum Airport in Calcutta, but also the serious humidity. You spend a lot of time trying to escape it – getting to the cool of air-conditioning in a hotel, to the cool of marble floors and the cool of a drink filled to the brim with ice. Mummy always said I shouldn't have ice because 'You never know if the water has been properly boiled first and it might upset your tummy'. Any food that I'm to eat cannot involve salad or rolls, as they're sure to give me a runny tummy too, as 'You don't know who has touched them'.

While stepping out of the aircraft onto the hot metal steps leading down to the melting tarmac, the heat is SO intense it almost knocks you off your feet. There are no buses into the airport terminal so it's a boiling walk with me still in my warm England garb – never properly prepared for the heat that is upon me. I arrive with my tin box of sweets courtesy of BOAC and am very grateful that I'm getting off at Calcutta. The plane is full of children flying further on to Singapore and Hong Kong, some even to Sydney, Australia.

DumDum Airport is chaos – the noise of people shouting, suitcases being dumped all dusty and battered, no conveyor belt – and there is my mother, always there – dependable. She elbows people out of the way when she sees me, her only child arriving for the summer holidays. After starchy hugs we rush outside to find our driver and our standard Ambassador car. All the cars are exactly the same in Calcutta. They're called Ambassador but are really the old Morris Oxford. Also, there's not much difference in their colour. They are white, black or cream. Taxis are yellow. Once, Daddy had a white Ford Zephyr, which was really special.

Our Ambassador is cream. We manoeuvre through the mess of traffic – there are no rules of the road here, the same Ambassador cars are everywhere, together with cows, goats, dogs and a huge cacophony of noise – everything assaults you and these are my favourite memories. There are buses too, our English red double-deckers, but somehow these Indian versions are unkempt and, to hide this, they have been decorated with flowers, lights, gold paint and all-sorts. These buses are the dregs, no longer viable in England, shipped out to continue their slow death in a country trying to find its independence and to get out of its old English majesty. Those onboard hang on to anything they can find. Hens in crates bounce on the roof held down by ropes attached to piles of sacks. Remarkably, I've never seen any of these buses fall over. How do they manage to move along the road to get through the teeming amount of activity that is just a normal day in Calcutta?

In those days Calcutta was a one-night stopover before catching a Fokker F27 Friendship plane up to the plains of Assam where my father would meet us at Tezpur Airport, essentially a dusty, concrete shed with a tin roof.

Eventually, Mummy and I reach a haven of peace in the middle of this heaving city. The Grand Hotel is possibly the grandest of them all, but it is on Chowringhee, one of the busiest roads in the city. You cannot believe that such an oasis exists in this incredible place where the smells, fumes, heat, petrol, engine noise and spice infatuate me even now. I haven't been back for so long that it actually hurts. Occasionally, in certain moments, something will trigger that strange, alluring aroma and I am transported back in time. Another of those nostalgic smells is tea, that deeply pungent smell you just can't get when you open a packet of supermarket tea bags. I don't know what they do to tea these days, I guess it's mixed up and, like with most other things, it just isn't the same. Putting tea in a bag takes the magic and smell away.

The Grand Hotel was pure luxury, from the marble pillars and entrance foyer of mosaic floor, to the liveried staff catering to your every need. You felt special the moment you walked in. I swam in the hotel's pool, which is oddly small and not in keeping with the majesty of the hotel itself. Once, I climbed into the wardrobe in our hotel bedroom and somehow locked myself in. I don't know why I would do such a thing! Poor Mummy was in such a panic and screamed down the telephone for help, which came soon enough. My mother was not a calm person and inclined to panic – neither was she a loving or huggy presence. Appearance was everything and to be seen to be doing what she considered the right thing.

On other occasions, Mummy and I would stay at the Fairlawns Hotel in Sudder Street, which has an old colonial grandeur but in a gently fading way. A hotel where everything – walls, iron pillars, chairs and tables – were painted green, which actually is quite a soothing colour. People would come here if they couldn't afford to stay at The Grand, but you wouldn't have considered the owner shy or retiring. She, Violet Smith, was considered rather eccentric. She inherited the house from her mother and was a typical colonial memsahib entertaining her many guests. Many famous people have passed through its portals – Felicity Kendall, Patrick Swayze and Julie Christie to name a few. The servants wore white gloves when serving you, apparently because old colonials did not like the sight of brown hands serving their food (this might have something to do with the reason my mother didn't think salads and bread rolls should be eaten?)

Chapter Seven

Returns to School

Since I only saw my parents during some of the school holidays, usually the long summer one, I would start crying two weeks before I was due to head back to England. I can't believe that my parents were actually going to put me back on the plane after all the fuss I'd make: 'It's OK, Penny darling, it really won't be long until we see each other again, and don't forget that we'll be able to bring you out much more regularly from now on', goes my mother. My imagination was having nightmares about the long drive to the airport at Tezpur and saying goodbye to Daddy. But that wasn't the worst of it. It was saying goodbye to my beloved dog, the dog that had now climbed into my going home suitcase and fallen asleep. I think it was because she knew I was going away and that made me cry even more. It was the wrench of leaving my dog and the tea gardens rather than saying goodbye to my parents. It was always so long and drawn out, what with Mummy and I staying overnight in Calcutta, then the drive to DumDum Airport and another long wait at departures, but at least my mother was allowed to come through as all unaccompanied children were allowed their parent at that time. But then there would be the long overnight flight back to Heathrow where Gaga would meet me. As I got older, I didn't get as upset about leaving as I used to.

There was one occasion on my many flights to Calcutta when I was sitting right at the back of the plane where smoking was allowed. An Indian gentleman sat next to me and asked, 'Would you like to see a party trick?'

'Ooh, yes please'. But no, it was not like that! He took his wine glass and covered it with his paper napkin, which he pulled tight across the glass and held down. He placed a small coin in the middle, lit a cigarette and we took it in turns to burn small holes in the tissue all around the coin. The trick is not to let the coin drop to the bottom of the glass on your go, but I did. I never played it again.

***

Jax is my best friend in the whole wide world and has been since she became a boarder at 11 years old. It was a bit touch and go with our friendship to begin with though as she was really popular with everyone. My best friend used to be Sarah whose parents were also in India, but as there weren't that many of us we all hung out together at different times and actually we are all still friends today.

Jax and I used to throw tennis balls against walls to catch, first one bounce, then two. Throw the ball and turn around to catch, under one leg, then the other. By the time I reached my early teens, I'm in both the lacrosse and tennis teams. We played cat's cradle with string around our fingers and we also created a parachute. We played endless games of jacks with metal objects. On school walks I would pick a thick blade of grass to hold between my thumbs, which would make a trumpet noise when I blew between them. There were other grasses that I picked with little black heads, which, when the stalk is wrapped around the head and pushed, it looks like an ant, so we'd call this 'flying ants'. Best of all were the séances in the cloakroom where we'd create our own Ouija board with the alphabet letters and 'Yes' and 'No' at either end. Jane said that if the glass fell into your lap you would be possessed by the Devil – scary stuff. All the above I teach my girls now except the séance bit.

My school friends and I would make up poems, including this one that ends up in the school magazine, *L'Alouette*:

'Silent sucking sounds in the dead drugged den
as the groupies grovelled to find more grass to sell themselves to sin.
The silent ticking of the clock as the hours slip away
and the sun slowly rises for the breaking of the day.'

We were allowed to stay up late on Thursday nights to watch *The Virginian*, a cool cowboy and Indian TV series. When I say 'stay up late', what I mean is later than 7pm, which is the time we were supposed to go to bed.

As the Easter holidays of 1969 drew to a close and before I was due to fly back, I contracted dengue fever and the brilliant news was that I couldn't return to school as scheduled. One minute I was boiling hot, the next I was shivering under the sheets and I couldn't do a proper poo. What I mean is that I had a huge desire to go to the loo but when I got there the desire had gone – apparently this is one of the symptoms. My bed had been wheeled out onto the veranda for a change of scene. A point of fact, I didn't feel that ill but I definitely didn't want to go back to school, not yet. This continued for two weeks and, strangely, became a happy time for me. My mother was very attentive, rubbing my back to help ease the difficulty and saying 'Poor darling, you are suffering; soon be better, though'.

Now that my father was a superintendent, instead of staying in hotels in Calcutta, my Mummy and I stayed in the penthouse suite at the top of the George Williamson & Co – later McNeil & Magor – head office. At the time it was the world's largest tea producing company. This was indeed luxury with a large roof garden overlooking the financial district of Calcutta, a heaving mess of cars, people, bicycles and noise. Just above the garden was the incredible tangle of electricity cables and phone wires dangling precariously – God knows how they got anything fixed or how anything worked! Inside up there was peace and almost absolute silence – a kind of respectfulness. With beautifully decorated and furnished rooms, comfy sofas and armchairs, a dining area with a highly polished mahogany table and chairs, it was all self-contained with its own servants and cook.

As I get older Mummy teaches me lots of games like mahjong, Canasta and Kalooki and we play a game of some sort every day when I'm home. The only time my father tried to teach me anything it was bridge and, don't ask, it was terrible. I cried.

As I've previously mentioned, I loved to swim and spend hours and hours underwater in the pool in my make-believe worlds. I could lose myself in water as I swam in my fairytales. At one corner I had a fantastical palace of mermaids and the other corner for the kings and queens. When you spend a lot of time underwater you are bound to hit trouble – in my case it was my ears. I'd get boils in my middle ear and then more in my inner ear. These would come once I'd returned to school after the summer holidays. Balance was a problem and the pain was something else. I spent a lot of time in the sick bay at the beginning of the school term.

***

Back at school, Miss White was a particular teacher who couldn't really control our class for toffee. She would lose her temper and send a variety of children to stand outside the room for the slightest misdemeanour. At February half term she'd gone skiing, returning with a broken arm, which never seemed to set properly, so from then on her left arm was always bent up and she never straightened it again.

From Avondale we moved on to Silverdale East, one of the two senior boarding houses. Even though we are still growing up, I am in a dormitory with six other girls. Local boys keep turning up and chucking pebbles at our dorm windows to attract our attention. We crowd round the window and gesticulate for them to go away but we don't really want them to.

Two of my roommates were Annabel and Connie and I am sorry to say I wasn't very nice to either girl. It wasn't so much as not treating them well I just ignored them as much as I could. One term, Annabel, a large girl, came back from the holidays with her leg in plaster. She would wet herself, the urine seeping down inside the plaster and making the stitches septic. When the plaster cast came off, the scar resembled deeply discoloured train tracks.

Chapter Eight

Calcutta

It's December 1970, my father has been promoted again and we are moving to Calcutta, leaving Phulbari Tea Estate and my entire life. I am being told this by my mother in one of her many airmail letters and I am not happy. I'm 14 years old, very sad and cross. What a wrench to say goodbye to Pugli our head bearer, Durjo our cherished driver and the rest. Although Loppy was still alive at this point, all our other pets are dead and buried in a paved off area and I'm sad at the thought of not being able to visit their graves. Goodbye to the swimming pool and the changing rooms that Daddy cleverly called 'Gulls' for girls and 'Buoys' for boys and his sign that read "Tis 'ere m'dear' ('It's here, my dear', which people thought was funny) for the shower. But I didn't get a chance to actually say goodbye to anything or anyone because I was not returning to Assam. (When I finally return in 2012 I forget to look for the pet cemetery but the changing rooms are exactly the same).

It turns out I love Calcutta, a heaving, teeming metropolis full of busyness and bustle and dust and filth and mess and muddle. It suits my personality which, when I think about it, is rather worrying.

At first there's no TV here either – although this comes eventually – and there are power cuts, which sometimes last for three hours or more. Our cook creates the most amazing dishes, with desserts all creamy meringue and spun sugar. I don't know how he knew so much about catering since my mother couldn't cook. I assume he must have picked up ideas from other British families he'd cooked for – he was already very old when he started working for us.

And there are parties galore, every night if you so desire. Dinners, drinks, more dinners, dances, more drinks and loads of kids my age as well. It was always the same people attending them. This irritated my father who would say, 'What's the point of this party? We're going to see the same people and will run out of things to talk about'.

Gina Cooch Behar is beautiful and resplendent in a sari, the only English woman I know who could wear the garment and look exotic and beautiful. I think I came across Gina at the Calcutta races. She married the maharaja of that name who had been killed on his polo pony and, although widowed, she was still young as she continued to play the part of a maharani living in a run-down house with a young man as companion. She was always drinking gin and tonic in a long glass with a paper napkin always held under the drink so that the glass didn't drip condensation. She caused quite a sensation wherever she went and gossip followed her everywhere, not least because of this young live-in stallion more than half her age in her rather large but bohemian house. Oh yes, I forgot, she was also having an affair with one of the fathers who worked in banking. His son became a good friend of mine.

It wasn't unusual for my parents to go to several parties in the one evening, starting off with drinks at 6pm. They would leave at 7.30–8pm to go somewhere else for dinner and then leave at 10pm for little soupçons of something such as a brandy at the club.

For a time, we lived in one section of a huge Georgian mansion at 22 Camac Street; us on one side with the larger part for visiting guests such as Michael Foot MP and Gerald Durrell. We had two peacocks in the garden and it was extraordinary that we were in the middle of a teeming city and yet all was peaceful there.

Both my parents had huge noses, which they kindly passed on to me. Goddamn it, of all the people they could have chosen to marry, they chose each other. It's funny how when you're young everything about you – especially your face – doesn't quite fit. My nose was ginormous and Pinocchio-like. In fact, nothing about me pleased me aged 14 and 15. I was flat-chested, my body was straight up and down and shapeless and my feet stunk to high heaven so much that Jax made me hang my socks and tights out the bedroom window. My hair was so messy, so no change there, but I was allowed to socialise with other children my age who were out for their summer holidays too. My social life in Calcutta was busy. There were just so many kids out there and we met up regularly at Tollygunge Club for swimming and Thums Up and I felt really grown up because I was allowed to sign for drinks and food because, as members, my parents got a monthly bill.

The rooms in Camac Street were enormous with exceedingly high ceilings. The veranda was enclosed by a beautiful wrought-iron carved surround – yes, we now had an enclosed veranda as well as a front door. Ceiling fans were commonplace and – whoopy-do – we had air-conditioning in every room. With the power cuts every day, Daddy liked to have the air-conditioning on ice mode so when the electricity went off the rooms stayed cooler for longer. Quite often I had to wear a cardigan, which was ridiculous in the 100°-plus heat outside and the 100 per cent humidity.

My parents continued to sleep in separate beds with a bedside table in-between. There was barely any affection between them although I never heard raised voices either. Someone said once that this is what happens after many years of marriage. Each of their double beds were handmade and my father slept while cuddling a pillow that he called his Dutch wife.

Now that we're in a city my mother has joined all sorts of charitable good works – the Women's Friendly Organisation, which promotes art and culture, employment and training for women; South Park Street Cemetery; British Association for Cemeteries in South Asia (BACSA)… all-sorts. These latter groups maintain and restore the many hundreds of European cemeteries, isolated graves and monuments in India, but my mother was mostly involved with the massive restoration of South Park Street Cemetery in Calcutta. There is a plaque dedicated to her there and it's quite a tourist attraction. Before India's independence, life was considered so hard on the British that it was generally thought that you would only last for two monsoons before dying.

My mother also joins the Botanical Society and anything to do with gardens and gardening, although she'd never actually get out there to do any actual hard gardening work, mind. She also managed to accidentally kill our two beautiful peacocks by putting down poison – I'm not sure what she was trying to poison.

She's also particularly interested in the United Kingdom Citizens Association for British women who have stayed on in India when their husbands have died. Others have chosen to stay on as couples but it's quite common for the husband to die first leaving the widow with no financial means of leaving India and no income because their husband's pension would have stopped at death. Apparently, there are lots of women stuck here. She's the secretary and is always off doing something good somewhere.

I'm not at home very often at this time so I can only get a glimpse of what she does, but her office is a complete mess of papers, dusty files and manual typewriters. She really ought to spend more time cleaning up her cupboards at home, which are also crammed full of ancient newspapers and cuttings to remind her about something that she will never refer back to. All these good works, though, add up to something and in 1985 she is awarded an MBE.

At Camac Street we don't have as many servants as we did in Assam, and once we moved to an apartment after about four years there was no need for malis as there was no garden to tend to. Krishna is our head bearer and is cherished by us, especially my mother who dotes on him. He speaks very good English, which is unfortunate for me because I really want to keep up my Hindi. At Camac Street we have the usual malis, cook and sweeper, and Krishna has someone working under him. We still have a dhobi wallah, but sadly Gwennie has retired and returned to Shillong and we have Mohammed, our driver – later, when I come out with Jax, we get a second driver, Jalil. Daddy paid for Gwennie to have some of her teeth capped in gold as her retirement gift and she receives a small pension.

Gwennie was always a gentle presence but stayed very much in the background. When I think about it, she reminds me very much of my ex-husband's mother. I have a surreal black and white photo, which shows my mother half-heartedly holding my hand, almost like she's holding a cup of tea with her pinky finger sticking out, and I'm dressed in a frothy party dress. In the immediate background is a boy playing with a balloon and, further back, is Gwennie standing in the shadows, carefully watching. My family didn't really go in for much hugging or chatting, but I always felt very much loved by Gwennie.

The formality of turbans and white starched uniforms disappears in Calcutta, where our servants are more casually clothed with loose-fitting khaki trousers and jackets, no turbans and bare feet. Krishna's family live in the south of India but he's worked for British companies for many years, well before my father's time. In the guest house next door, there's John bearer – and always referred to as such. He has much darker skin than our other bearers, with perfectly spoken English in an almost upper-class tone. He's head of the guest household and you'd be mistaken for thinking that he was privately educated in England. It's incredible that they live their own lives so far apart from their families, only seeing them once a year when my parents go home for annual leave.

The bottom line with all our servants is their faithfulness. They speak quietly and everything about them is gentle and good, plus they're all so bloody accommodating – nothing is too much trouble and, even though we let them go at 9pm, that's still late when you consider that Krishna has to be up early to fetch my parents' breakfast tea.

Today, 22 Camac Street has been knocked down and rebuilt to become a modern shopping mall.

On leaving Camac Street, my parents found themselves living in splendid surroundings at The Bengal Club for four months until the apartment at Judges Court Road in Alipore district was ready. They had a suite of rooms and I immediately want to sit up straight as I write this because of the formality of the club. One had to dress for dinner, but what I remember most were the boring meals as there was never any change to the menu – I just remember eating a lot of sole meunière. I'm not there that often but when I am at Christmas time for my four-week holiday, sole meunière every bloody night becomes tedious!

Eventually we move to 10 Judges Court Road, a horrid-looking red-brick building of a block of flats, but the apartments inside are sumptuous as you would expect: Three bedrooms, three bathrooms, air-conditioning everywhere with an elevator to bring you to your floor and directly into your apartment – but there are still power cuts. Jimbo, our intricately carved huge wooden elephant greets visitors in the small hall before you approach double doors to enter the flat itself. Immediately in front of you are McNeil and Magor, the two large brass storks, called that because you may remember the company Daddy worked for has had a change of name and ownership. A small passageway opens onto the dining room. There is a formal sitting room in the middle and to the right a snug room where my parents and I relax in the evenings. Each room is divided up by carved wooden screens which give the impression they are much bigger because you can see all three rooms – dining, formal sitting and snug – at once.

I am in serious party mode these days, although I realise I have to pay some attention to my parents so will stay in with them to play cards, have supper at 9ish and then get Mohammed to drive me either to someone's house for a party or to meet everyone at the cricket club on the maidan. The maidan is pronounced 'mydarn' and is the green lung of Calcutta, a vast area watched over by the beautiful Victoria Memorial. I'm often not home until the wee small hours.

I don't know how our driver copes and I'm embarrassed that I keep him up so late because at 15/16/17 years old I'm always out. When I run out of cigarettes, all I have to do is send Mohammed to get me some more. It's usually about 2am that I send him out and rarely am I home before 4am. I'm so unthinking because the poor man has to be back at our apartment to drive Daddy to work for 8am. I am at the height of selfishness. Later on, towards the end of my father's time, Mohammed becomes very religious and whenever it's prayer time he stops the car – doesn't matter where – and jumps out to pray to Mecca.

Many times I'd end up at David's chummery – a flat shared with other tea assistants who are learning the tea trade. It was two streets from my parents' flat and I'd walk home in the misty early hours with a bra hanging out of my bag, looking a little dishevelled, only to find my father about to leave for the office. He never said a word as I slunk off to bed. I'm grateful for that.

In the morning, it's the usual tea and lemon in hot water for my mother at 6am, make-up on and breakfast at 7am. My father's breakfast consists mainly of the previous day's tea, fried with an egg thrown in, and cigarettes. When I'm there it's 'wake Penny at nine' time – 'Oh God, darling, your breath smells!' says Mummy as she draws back my curtains, and oh God it's too bright. Go back and wake Penny at 10. Go back and wake Penny at 11, 'last time now, darling'. Off she then goes to volunteer with all the charity work she's involved with until 1pm. I wake up gingerly with a roaring headache realising I mustn't be grumpy in front of my parents and wondering how I'm going to stay awake all day and go out again tonight. Lunch at 1.15 prompt, siesta until 2.20 – oh bliss, I'd forgotten I could get a little shut-eye – tea at 4.30 and then await my father's arrival at 5pm. At 5.30 Krishna removes my father's shoes in exchange for his slippers and at 6pm my father says to Krishna, 'Bring me my medicine, please'. At 6.05 a pink gin is duly delivered.

So here we have Krishna who has a junior bearer under him, then a cook and a gooselkarma boy. The gooselkarma (bath boy/cleaner and, yes, he runs our baths for us) is still low caste and although I will say good morning or hello to him, we don't converse; he lowers his eyes to the floor, which is not far away as he's usually on his haunches cleaning them. No change there, then.

***

My mother always did the right thing or perhaps what *she* thought was the right thing. She always had to make sure that what she considered to be the Queen's English was spoken and that the table was laid. It wasn't until I became a teenager and the late developer that I was did I realise how crass my mother's attitude was. Taking an elevator/lift, for instance, in Calcutta: Say there was a crowd of us, my mother and I and also an Indian family, all waiting for that lift at the same time and we can all fit in easily. My mother (and I am so ashamed about this) would literally push her way into the elevator FIRST. My mother felt she was above those Indians and would instruct me, 'Come along, Penny darling'. She had to be the first person to walk into the lift and this is the woman who was born in India and lived most of her life there.

If I told my mother that I liked a certain dish like cottage pie for instance, then this would be served up every single day until I was sick at the sight of it. Our cook (bobbachee) would make tiny, crustless, tomato sandwiches sprinkled with sugar for teatime and always beautifully presented – I'm salivating as I write this.

My poor mother, as I have already said and to prove the point further, she really was a stickler for 'doing the right thing', the 'U' and 'non-U' of doing things ('U' being the correct way of doing/ saying things and 'non-U' being the opposite. This is from a book called *Noblesse Oblige* edited by Nancy Mitford). In other words, table manners were also very important. For instance, one mustn't scoop peas onto an upturned fork. No. Peas must be edged up and onto the top of the fork, prongs facing down and... really? It was impossible and *why do I have to eat like this?* You mustn't tip your bowl of soup towards you to eke out the last dregs. Instead, one must tip the bowl away from one and do the same with the spoon, scooping it away from the front of the bowl to the back. When I questioned this stupidity, Mummy said it was in case the soup fell into your lap by mistake – but it's the last smattering of it!

Under no circumstances were you to sprinkle salt all over your food either, it had to be put in a neat pile on the side of your plate for the purpose of food to be taken to the pile and dipped into. Then there was my enunciation at the dinner table – 'it's not 'yeow', darling, it's 'yoo yoo yoo''. And 'for goodness sake, do not hold your knife as though it is a pen'.

This is my mother, the traditional ex-pat wife, the stay-at-home wife, except she doesn't really stay at home with all her good works and who is the ruler of the home roost. My mother's jaw clicked when she chewed, which I'm pretty sure isn't 'U'.

As I grow up to pursue more adult-like pursuits as it were, I find I can go into a street stall and buy just one cigarette. Before I fly back to England, I will buy 200 of my favourite red Marlboros on the black market and still cheaper than the duty-free at the airport. A little boy is given a few paise to climb up a hollowed out tree to get them from their hiding place.

***

At 16, all six of us in the senior year are prefects, some of us having to double up on prefect duties because, well, there are only six of us in the whole year. This really should have been a huge advantage, but of course we just mucked around. Jax and I are joint heads of choir and drama. Really, we are so irresponsible that I'm sure it was a stretch for us to be considered at all.

The following year we are finally deemed old enough to have our own bedrooms, which are in what would have been the attic for servants in the old days. My room is next to Jax's with a fire escape on the other side of the passageway that is incredibly useful and a great entry point for our boyfriends to sneak up. It is brilliant fun. Jon and Richard cycle over in the dead of night and we'd have a good few hours snogging and you-know-what – but not too much – then they cycle back.

The food was disgusting at the PNEU – tapioca pudding, which we called frogs' eggs because that's what it looked like – fried eggs all gloopy with the white not cooked properly. Thames mud, though, was a delicious enough chocolate mousse pudding with a crunchy oat topping. Whatever the quality of the food, I was always hungry and wanting seconds and so had to down my meal very quickly in time for more. At that time our boarding house was having central heating installed and thus a lot of building work was ongoing. There were three workmen and it was a bit of a muddle at first because I liked Mark but he liked Caro; Jax ended up with Bill and I was with Steve. We didn't end up *together* together, we just sneaked out to the pub on occasions. We three girls always stuck together, but after the last occasion in the pub, I was called into the headmistress' study. It turns out I'd been seen in the pub with Steve. No mention of Jax and Caro who were also present at the same time. Well, all hell broke loose and it was decided the whole sixth form – all six of us – would go to see the headmistress together – that was such a nice thing of them to do. She was called Mrs Harford and wore her grey hair up in a chignon. One of her legs was straight but the other arched alarmingly round from the shin.

Once we were all sitting down facing our serious headmistress, she began. 'You know I have a daughter called Penny', she said, 'and she is now married to a builder...' She burst into tears, clearly upset at this union. Well, you could have knocked me over with a feather except I was already sitting down. There was the threat of telling my mother and the warning that if this sort of thing happened again she would have no choice but to expel me. It was a bit of an anticlimax after all the build-up.

I just didn't give education enough attention and I didn't have anyone to tell me to concentrate, least of all my school. I'd study for each O-level exam the night before while listening to Georges Moustaki that my friend Doodie introduced me to. When I get only 13 per cent in my mock maths, it's a huge relief to be able to give it up. Even today, my brain just isn't geared up for any kind of adding or taking away. I did love history though, but we only learnt about the Tudors and Stuarts, so with so few qualifications and a ton of retakes, I feel thick. The only sex education I had at school was how rabbits got to have babies, so really there's little hope for me. I haven't a clue.

I write to my parents once a week on a blue airmail letter form and sometimes it is such a struggle to fill it up. My mother, on the other hand, writes to me at least three times a week. We were much better conversing via letter than face to face. Her letters were really chatty, perhaps about who had been over the previous evening for a dinner party and, more likely, who had been at the races that weekend. Perhaps she was going to have an evening dress made and she'd tell me about going for a fitting.

Chapter Nine

Teenage Times

There's quite a crowd of us younger generation who get together in the summer holidays. We go to the cinema where I do wish Bruce would stop faffing about trying to find my tits, which at this time are the main attraction among all the necklaces that I wear. This is a time of patchouli joss sticks and patchouli everything, frankly, or we'd turn up at each other's houses and just hang out, *man*. There was always a party to go to – sometimes with our parents – as well as horse racing and polo on a Saturday. For us teenagers there really was a kind of opulence to our lives.

I bring out fashion magazines from England and select a few designs, which our dressmaker Morsalem (durzi) will knock together in under a week – all from a tiny hut on a busy, filthy street on a battered old Singer foot pedal-operated sewing machine. There is a little corner curtained off so I can try things on, which isn't as easy as you'd imagine. With no cool air and pouring with sweat it's a struggle to get in and out of dresses.

I love to visit the New Market and most days that is where you would find me with my basket boy, Ashraf. It is a rabbit warren of a place and huge – well, not huge in its height, but wide. It's not a good idea to attempt to walk around it on your own. It's crammed full of every kind of shop you could wish for – there's a jewellery stall (Chumba Lumba), another V Gulab & Sons and another with beautiful silks and saris. They are draped over horizontal poles that gently blow in the draughts created by the punkas – or fans. But it's dusty. Young boys sweep the ground, merely moving the dust and dirt from one side to the other, then the dust rises and my mother turns fiercely to me and instructs, 'Breathe out, Penny darling, breathe out now!' She was forever dreading that if I breathed in I would pick up some horrible disease.

If you do decide to shop in the New Market on your own, shopkeepers accost you every step of the way enticing you to shop at their stall. 'Ay Missahib, you come to my shop, I give you good price, ay ay'. Once you'd found a regular basket boy they would look out for you to arrive and generally look after you to make sure you didn't get ripped off. They do have their special shops where, if you buy from it, the boy would get a tip.

Beggars are everywhere and they will come and tap on your car windows if you're stuck in a traffic jam, which is pretty much all the time. Mummy says that their parents had maimed most beggars shortly after birth so that they could be sent out to beg – it's horrid. There was a woman whose neck was stretched raw. She had just a hole for a mouth and no nose, just two holes. There were some terrible sights and it's so difficult to ignore the tapping, touching and pulling of my dress as I move through the crowds.

***

We are given quite a lot of freedom for a boarding school. There's a school dance, which has been resurrected after a few years because, so the story goes, one of the girls got pregnant at the last one. Ours takes place in the school hall with students from Hurstpierpoint College, Lancing College and Christ's Hospital, which is an actual school and not, as the name suggests, a hospital. The hobnail boots the boys from Christ's Hospital are wearing ruins the highly polished floor. On another occasion a few of us visit Lancing College where the band Genesis are playing, and I get to see some of it. I can't believe I opted to stay in gorgeous Barry's study instead, but there you go, he *is* gorgeous.

By this time Jax and her older sister, Manda, have moved into a one-bedroom flat in a village within cycling distance from school. In fact, the whole building is made of one-bed flats – a hall, kitchen, bathroom and then upstairs to a sitting room and up another staircase to a bedroom. These are the days of bouncing on the sofa bed to Noddy's Bouncing Ball Town, which, to our teenage ears, was all about boys with balls and innuendo, wetting yourself funny, crowds of people flowing in and out, nights of telling ghost stories and scaring myself shitless, smoking, more smoking, crazy times with Graham and his brother dressing up in pink negligees and us wearing seven pairs of knickers as we all fall helplessly on the sofa bed, eventually comatose.

Manda used to be known as the Gin Queen because that was her daily tipple in the North Star pub – gin and orange, no ice. I tell her that I reckon she was my mother in a previous life because, although she is only four years older than me, she has a certain maturity about her and she talks a lot of sense – well, she talks a *lot*. As we get older Manda and Jax become more like sisters to me and seem more of a family than my own one, excluding my own children of course. Apart from both talking a lot, Manda and Jax are the polar opposite of each other.

***

I'm now 17 years old and feeling confident, grown up. I'm nervous too, though, because I've decided to tell my parents that I smoke. I'm going to lie a bit and say I only smoke at parties – ha! I'd rather not say anything and I know Daddy won't mind as he smokes morning, noon and night, but Mummy will go mad. Crap! This time Jax is coming out too because school is over forever – yay! Jax is going to spend some of the holiday with me for a couple of weeks before going off to Kalimpong Homes to volunteer.

During those two weeks when Jax is out, we drive down to Puri for a long weekend. The company has a beautiful bungalow that we stay in often. Puri is 300 miles out of Calcutta and takes a whole day to get there by car. Sometimes we – my parents and I that is – go by train, which was always dead exciting because it involved station porters balancing our suitcases and picnic basket atop their turbaned heads. I loved to observe everything and enjoyed sleeping on the train, too. It was an all-night journey. We started off sitting on the leather-covered compartment benches and having our picnic – a hard-boiled egg each, plain cheese sandwiches and lashings of Thums Up. At some point, the train bearers would arrive with pristine white sheets to turn our benches into bunk beds.

This time we are travelling by car with Mohammed, leaving in the morning and hoping to arrive by evening. The bungalow at Puri looked quite majestic in a small house way. It was right on the beach but you wouldn't dare walk anywhere on the sand with bare feet – it was boiling.

The waves here in the Bay of Bengal are seriously serious, so much so that it is impossible to get into the sea without holding onto a beachboy. It's usually an old man who is incredibly toned and strong. They wear conical raffia hats to indicate who they are.

The bedrooms have mosquito nets draped around the beds and really the whole setting of this house is romantic. It is a gentle time where there's nothing more taxing to think about other than what card game to play later and looking forward to a rum and coke – sorry Thums Up – later.

These days there are times when I can take myself straight back to India, especially on a dark, hot summer's night. There's a certain aroma, not just of joss sticks but that tropical heat that I sense as I lie in this bed beside my eight-year-old sleeping daughter. My ears buzz and I imagine I'm hearing the cicadas – that constant and evocative tropical sound. I hear the cars rushing up the high street and, if I take my imagination up a huge step in a weird direction I imagine the traffic sound is really the thudding of ocean waves on sand. I'm in Puri.

Chapter Ten

Feeling Posh

It is 1973 and I'm about to start finishing school at Winkfield Place near Windsor. It is the crème de la crème of finishing schools. I learn how to arrange flowers, cordon bleu cooking and how to sew (oh, please, no). My mother's two main reasons for me attending this most prestigious of places is firstly, that I'll meet an eligible bachelor, preferably someone with a title and, secondly, that I'll learn shorthand and typing which are always useful skills – something 'one can fall back on' as Mummy says. My mother's plan is to turn me into a young lady and by sending me to Winkfield Place she is assured of that.

The scary thing is that everyone is really posh, total Hooray Henriettas. All these 'gels' have private incomes and, as I discover during the year I'm there, they purchase a new wardrobe for every season. My allowance is £50 per term, which really doesn't go very far and I'm nearly always in debt by the end. Trips to Harvey Nicks, Harrods and designer stores were normal for them. I hadn't got a clue what they were on about. Despite their love of luxury clothing, their ambitions were mundane: 'After here I'm going to study History of Art in Italy, you know' or, 'I'll probably go and work in Harrods', but really, none of them had to do a proper job. I was different. I *had* to get a job and so, having spent years of schooling not really pushing myself to any great degree, I decide I am going to work really hard on my secretarial skills and see if I can make my parents proud, my mother mostly.

There are two streams to choose. The first is concentrated on the cordon bleu cookery side with a bit of secretarial thrown in. The second is mostly secretarial with cordon bleu and other stuff thrown in. I choose the latter. We sit in rows in front of manual typewriters with a plastic cover over the letters and endlessly practise touch-typing. The cooking must have rubbed off on me somewhere along the line because it turns out I can cook quite well, but don't talk to me about bloody sewing! I recently bought a sewing machine, however, which I intend to start up one day.

I'm with a group of really nice girls who have names like Camilla Smythe and Cordelia Double-Barrel Something. I'm really here to become a lady, since it is my mother's intention that I will marry someone rich with a title. I'm not doing too badly on that score actually because I've been with my boyfriend Jon since school.

We met when our schools joined forces to put on Shakespearean plays. I was in *The Comedy of Errors* and Jon was in the audience. I played the courtesan: 'Now out of doubt, Antipholus is mad, else would he never so demean himself...' We put the play on in modern dress so, for the courtesan part, I wore a tiny miniskirt, high-heeled strappy shoes and floppy hat. Best of all I had a long cigarette holder and was allowed a real ciggie at the end of it.

I've acquired rather long legs and enormous tits (in real life I hasten to add – not for the play!) An actual figure – no longer straight up and down. Afterwards, Jon comes backstage, we get talking and, basically, I can't believe anyone would fancy me and he's really good-looking. Jon's father is the Lord Mayor of London and is an actual Lord, which makes Jon an Honourable. You can imagine how pleased my mother is at the time. We've been together two years and just had proper sex for the first time at Rick's place in Bromley (he's Jax's boyfriend) and afterwards I sit wrapped up in a sheet watching *Department S*, a British spy-fi adventure series, on the telly.

At Winkfield we are ensconced in huts. My hut has four bedrooms and a bathroom at the end of the short corridor. I'm sharing a room with Melanie and Susie, and there's Camilla who shares the room opposite, and Fiona to the left of us. It's not so much about learning to be a lady but rather how to find a man to marry. None of these girls come close to becoming a lady I have to say, and their backgrounds, seemingly so gilded, are really down to earth.

Poor Camilla had a terrible experience. She was caught having sex with a boy in one of the ditches at the edge of the grounds. Her parents were informed and that weekend when she went home, and to teach her a lesson, her parents had sex in the sitting room in front of a roaring fire and made Camilla watch. That'll teach her. The things people do!

The girls at Winkfield wear dainty pearl earrings and always a pearl necklace. My mother buys me one but I don't need earrings since the girls in my dorm clubbed together and bought me a pair for my birthday.

I plan to have a bloody ball in the year I'm there and, even though I'm not a debutante as most of the girls plan to be, I'm invited and tag along to the many dos that their parents organise for their precious young things. There are tea parties and cocktail parties, better known as 'cocker Ps'. There are dinners, dances and – the highlight of the season – Queen Charlotte's Ball, an extravaganza extraordinaire. All 'coming out' debutantes that year, my year, are dressed in white ball gowns because you couldn't come out unless you were in virginal white. I was dressed beautifully, as it happens, in a long, deep sea-green dress of pure silk. It was floaty and, frankly, gorgeous. It had been copied from a photograph in *Vogue* magazine that I'd taken out to Calcutta during the previous term's holiday and which my faithful dressmaker, Morsalem, had followed precisely. He worked out of a bamboo hut on stilts in the middle of a busy street. The street was full of traders selling cigarettes by the singular and paan, a green leaf with a spicy/tangy flavour wrapped around betel nuts and white paste, by the singular, too. I loved it, but chewing it left my mouth red and made it very difficult to explain to my exasperated mother how my mouth got that colour. She thought it terribly unhygienic having food handed to you directly by the seller. It's why she never let me eat lettuce, salad items or bread rolls unless we were eating at home, 'because you don't know who's been touching it'.

How he and his assistants did their incredible work I'll never know, but I have huge respect for the end result. There were also other such wonderful treats to eat like jellabees, bright orange with a crisp outside and all liquidy in the middle. Sweet and delicious, they will bring on diabetes in an instant. You can still buy them these days at Brick Lane Market, but I've digressed...

***

Back at Queen Charlotte's Ball, we all sit at round tables, a long list of names is read out and each girl in white parades dutifully up to curtsey... when suddenly I hear my name. Oh my God. *WHAT?* I can't go up! I'm in bloody green, for Christ's sake. There is a flurry of panic and the moment passes.

I learn how to make a roux and how to find the tender oysters under the chicken. I make a halterneck dress and a hat to match. That's a lie; I didn't make the hat. That was a last-minute panic situation from my teacher who didn't think my halterneck dress was good enough to put on show. She found me a frustrating student. I'm really quite good at shorthand and the old typing on the manual typewriter and I also learn how to flower arrange, although these days I tend to fling everything into a vase, hope for the best and then notice that it actually looks all right.

Chapter Eleven

Working

By 1974, aged 18, I was working for a meat marketing company in Knightsbridge having just qualified as a junior secretary. My job involved taking dictation from the deputy to the company secretary, Colonel Roper, who was 54 but who behaved as if he was 100. Army chap indeed, but very nice and in those days I was treated rather fondly – you know, as you would your Labrador dog. I'm sure he had one of those, too. Isn't it funny how life has changed *so* much? Colonel Roper (and always addressed as such even though he was no longer in the army) came in by train from up country. I don't know how long he had been with the company, but retirement was in his sights and his life was gentle, or perhaps genteel. Everyone else was so serious though, no joy and excessively formal.

I am a fast typist and I also do shorthand, which in itself is like a completely different language. So, I'm tri-lingual if you count my mixture of Bengali and Assamese. The offices are right next door to the National Farmers' Union (NFU) in Knightsbridge, all glass and glitter. The Spaghetti House restaurant is just down the road where just a year later there was a siege and a gunman took six waiting staff hostage. I go there quite a lot because they serve lasagne, which I can have with ketchup. Jax comes up to London and we do the Ministry of Silly Walks down Knightsbridge and say things like, 'Ooh, you are awful, but I like you'. It was the days of Monty Python and short, short miniskirts. Jax and I are the coolest of cool. We carried on with this down in Sussex, too, where she and her big sister live.

Sometimes at the weekends I would help friends out on their Portobello Market stall where they sold jeans. On occasion they also employed a Saturday girl. They once sent her, with much giggling on their part, to the bakery to buy some dildos. They thought she was naïve – little did they know I had no idea what a dildo was either.

There was no pressure in the staid environment of the meat marketing company. I just typed the day away, bang, bang, bang, sliding in a Tipp-Ex paper to erase the letters I'd mistyped, together with the carbon copies, the blue ink of which gets all over your hands and then onto everything else. Eventually I was provided with an Olivetti electronic typewriter. I could be terribly light-fingered with this, which brought its owwwwwn problems – backspace four for 'W' –bloody hell. This is how the old Olivetti typewriters were like – to Tipp-Ex out an 'M' for instance was backspace three spaces and an 'N' was two back spaces…

After almost a year of endless typing and little joy, I developed a cough. At the time I was sharing a flat with my great friend Sarah and was almost a Sloane Ranger, don't you know! Even though I had the pearls, I couldn't abide velvet Alice bands and, anyway, I rarely walked down Sloane Street. Nevertheless, those were the days of the Sloane Ranger – frightfully posh accents, dark blue suits and cocktail parties.

Eventually, the cough became so severe I couldn't walk any distance without coughing uncontrollably, losing my breath and ending up burping in order to be able to breathe again. Lovely! So embarrassing! My job has become humdrum and sharing both an office and a flat with Sarah – my boyfriend Jon was friends with her boyfriend – was possibly not a good combination. I feel totally inferior to her, in fact to anyone who is older than me or senior to me at work, which is basically everyone, because I'm the junior. Actually, this is a theme that runs through my life. In those days, my constant inner refrain was that I wasn't good enough and, damn it, I wish I could get over myself instead of running myself down all the time. I drive myself crazy and what with the constant coughing, I'm a mess and at the end of my tether.

Colds and coughs had been a constant in my life from a young age. Mummy said it was because I had sinus trouble, which was why – aged 15 – I went into a nursing home somewhere near Worthing to have my sinuses taken out. I'm not sure if anyone explained exactly what this procedure would involve but I do remember being put to sleep and waking up some time later wondering why nothing had been done. I then turned my head to see Gaga sitting there, had an overwhelming need to be sick, which I was all over Gaga, and then leaving the two tubes hanging from my nose and mouth covered in horrid sticky bits. I had to breathe through my mouth and when I looked in the mirror I saw that my nose was bunged up with bloodstained cotton wool as well as the tubes. Of course, the tubes can't stay in my nose forever and, sure enough, a day or so later the strapping big-bosomed Sister comes bowling in and says, 'Now dearie, I'm just going to remove the tubes by giving them a gentle tug; it won't hurt at all...' *Hmmmm*. Well, I cried and would have sworn if I'd known the words to use.

So, you'd think that after that operation and the one when I had my tonsils removed aged seven, I wouldn't get so many colds and coughs? Flip, no. I just can't shake this persistent cough. I felt well though and continued to work, feeling rather confused about it all. I would cough during the short walk from the office to the tube. From the tube ticket office to the tube itself, I coughed, and from the tube station to my shared flat I coughed. It was exhausting and I realised I couldn't go on like that. I went to the doctor but no joy. No cough mixture would cure my cough.

In my younger days, and if I was feeling low, my feel-good thing was not to go shopping to buy something new, but rather to visit a clairvoyant. My first visit to such a person was in my lunch hour down a back street in Marble Arch. I entered the house, walked up a dark staircase and came to a red, velvet curtain which, when pulled back, revealed a room containing a round table. The room was dark and gloomy and a small, rotund older chap greeted me who announced I should take a seat and await the entrance of his wife, Madame. Shortly afterwards she came in, all whiskered and smelly with a black shawl around her rather rotund shoulders. I did feel spooked but after an hour's worth of speculation and her imaginings (or was it her ability to foretell my future?) I came out feeling a lot better than when I went in.

So, when I couldn't shake off the cough, I decided to consult my clairvoyant. Madame was amazing. She looked at me and said, 'Dear, you don't have a black shadow behind your head. If you did, I would certainly say you are ill and it would be something I could not help you with because you would need to see a doctor. Do you understand, dear? What it is is that you are unhappy in your job and your situation there. You need to go back to your company and resign immediately, and when you've done that you will find that you no longer have a cough'.

I was a little sceptical but believed her – except one didn't do that in those days. I couldn't go back to the office and resign on the spot without having something else – another job to go to. After all, I had rent to pay. You wouldn't believe it but in those days – the mid 70s – I earned £1,100 a year. This comfortably paid the £40 a month rent on my flat – I shared with two other friends and that sum included electricity, gas, etc – plus my travel and food.

Coughing, though, was not attractive and making me thin and nervy. So, on my way back to the office I thought and thought and then put in my resignation. I am not making this up when I say that when I went to catch my tube that evening, I no longer had my cough. How does that work?

The Executive Secretarial Bureau was just down the road from the office and I got a job straightaway. Since I felt that I was 'only a secretary', that's what I apply for and am employed as secretary to the company secretary of an electronic wholesalers in Buckingham Gate, Victoria. A step up, eh? The company is right over the road from Buckingham Palace and I have no idea what they're all about, but I like the other girls and I like my boss, Tim.

Basically, there is the chairman and his PA, the managing director and his PA, my boss, our receptionist, Charlie, and myself, except my boss doesn't seem part of the main set-up. For starters we're up on the third floor, which happens to be what would have been the loft. Tim and I have just two rooms and my boss is really young, sort of early 30s, whereas the chairman and MD appear older. Their PAs are gorgeous and give the impression of being so sophisticated.

Life is soon good again. I still have an Olivetti typewriter and I know how it works now, but I'm getting the impression that the other two PAs have a more intimate knowledge of their chairman and the MD. After eight months, my boss Tim starts to say, 'Come and sit on my lap for dictation'. I'm too naïve to understand and so I sit on his lap and I'm not sure if I can say no. This happens over and over and I don't like it but don't know what to do. At 10 months in the job I need to get away but know it won't look good on my CV to have moved again. One Monday, I ring the Executive Secretarial Bureau and say, 'I'm sorry, but please can you find me a job?' It doesn't take long but, in the meantime, Tim becomes even more demanding: a kiss in the morning, dictation on his lap and a kiss in the evening. I am not happy – but I still don't develop a cough – and then I get the best of jobs. Thank God the new company were quick off the mark when I told them of my little problem and got a verbal reference from Tim while I was still employed there. After that, I told him to stop.

Chapter Twelve

Memories

This is where my memory gets hazy as I can't remember if I moved into the Earl's Court flat before moving to the one just off Kensington High Street or the other way round. If Earl's Court came first, that would make sense because I was sharing a room with Anne who was at finishing college with me.

Anyway, at some point I ended up in a basement flat in Lennox Gardens, Earl's Court, and you could smell this flat from all the way down the road. There were pots and pans, mouldy leftovers, grease and dirt all piled high in the tiny kitchen whose sole window looked up and out to the street above. Smells rise. I needed a roof over my head and Anne said I could share her room. She said the flat was owned by a boy and 'sorry about all the mess'.

There was a large glass-topped coffee table in the front room and on it were lines and lines of white powder. The boy wore leather trousers with his front zip undone. I wasn't sure why and I had no idea about the white powder. I was more concerned about the lack of hygiene and set about cleaning and clearing the kitchen, which took forever, especially since there was no room for things to be stored.

I was also worried because my father was coming to London for a meeting and said he'd very much like to see where I was living. Oh, crumbs! I got busy trying to find a way to stop him from even coming down my street because the smell was that bad. Things didn't go well and when he arrived – thank God the boy was out – he announced that he would pay me to leave this godforsaken place and asked how the hell I could stay there. I learned later that the boy was part of the Hells Angels' Earl's Court Chapter. Oh right, that's okay then.

I don't recall how I left or how long after that conversation it was, but my next flat was up a massive flight of stairs, with no lift, around the back of Kensington High Street. Fab! I have Biba just down the road and Ken High Street is busy, busy, busy. There is just one small problem in that this flat has no sitting room. It has a hall, a kitchenette, a bathroom and two bedrooms. I share with two other girls who I never see. They're in one bedroom and I have the other, which is also the landlord's room. He says he won't intrude (well, thanks!) but he does have a chest of drawers in my room where he keeps some clothes and shoes. He says he's a film director and maybe I should have taken more notice because I could have been a famous actress by now if I'd thought about it. He kept turning up late at night and knocking on my door ostensibly to collect some items or something, but definitely with the true intention of trying to get into my knickers!

I'm still seeing Jon at this stage. He drives a white Fiat Sport Coupé, which has a sticker on the rear window saying 'Happiness is a soft pussy', but he doesn't ever find my pussy. On the weekends, when I'm not working at the market, I go down to Tadworth, Surrey, where my Jon is living in what was probably the gamekeeper's cottage on a large estate. I loved these weekends, every one of them sunny. Janine, whose boyfriend, Mick, was sharing this cottage with Jon, would often be there too and would make the most glorious omelettes. I still wasn't brave enough for cooking. There was music and strumming of guitars and a grand piano in the bedroom, but no sex – we didn't do sex. We were best friends, though. I'm not sure I realised that there should have been a bit of sex when you're in a boyfriend/girlfriend relationship, but it's all quite a blur and I can only imagine how naïve I must have been having attended an all girls' boarding school and an all girls' finishing school. I was soon on the move to another flat, this time in Paddington.

"No, darling, it's Bayswater."

"But, Mummy, it's just around the corner from Paddington tube."

Honestly, she's such a snob. My parents had recently bought a top floor flat around the corner from bloody Paddington Station and my tiny studio flat was two roads further away above a butcher's shop. My flat consisted of a sitting room, bedroom, a kitchen with Formica-top tables and a grubby bathroom that was down some stairs. Everywhere smelt bad because the woman below me had about 20 cats (a slight exaggeration, it was only five but felt like 20) and left milk out for them which, on hot days, became completely rancid. She was pretty rancid herself, an alcoholic, heavy smoker and permanently attired in a raggy old dressing gown. Then there was the smell from the butcher's…

My first love, Jon, often stays over and sometimes brings his friend Richard. This was a time for Ouija boards and play but no sex. I'm pretty sure this isn't normal so I try to get sexy and buy a set of baby-doll pyjamas, which were all the rage then. It still doesn't work and we remain best friends.

Jon told me a story once about how, when he was at school, he and a few boys decided to set up a Ouija session. After the usual 'Is anyone there?' the answer came back in the affirmative and the letters spelled out 'JON'. 'Who are you?' was asked and the answer came back, 'JFK'. It turned out that John F Kennedy knew Jon because he shook the hand of the boy next to Jon back at prep school. The boys were also told that MaryJo Kopechne was murdered by his brother Ted Kennedy, a United States senator, a secret the boys were asked never to divulge.

On another session, we were told never to visit Cranleigh because if we did, something bad would happen. It's just a place, a village near Guildford. It's strange that JFK would pick a random place like Cranleigh! To this day though, I have never been there. Jon did though. We eventually split up, he got a new job and the most convenient place to move to was Cranleigh. We didn't stay in touch so I've no idea if something bad did actually happen.

Then there was the time a message came through: 'Namaste Penny' ('namaste' being the customary Hindu greeting). I immediately burst into tears; I think it was Gwennie.

Chapter Thirteen

My Hair and Boys

My parents are about to come home to the UK for their annual six-week leave. They've already had their local leave of two weeks spent either in Shillong or camping with friends. I'm nervous because they're just two roads away from my flat and I'm shacked up with Jon. They could turn up at any moment. I don't have a phone. Jon and I agree that he will move back in with his mate Richard and I'm busy checking everywhere, mainly for stray socks. But after that smelly summer of cats, stale milk and hanging meat downstairs, he never moves back in and I move out too.

When my parents are home for their leave, they really want me to live with them so they can see me as much as possible. I find it hard saying no and move in, but it's difficult losing my independence and having to be back at a certain time. I resort to being a child again.

My mother didn't get married until she was 35 so she was dead keen for me to marry Jon, but our relationship by this stage was pretty stagnant. After four-and-a-half years together he left me for a girl called Mercedes. Rusty bloody minivan more like, which is what he drove.

I am 20 years old and beside myself with grief for the loss of my first love. I don't like my hair because of that tufty bit on top where Hilly randomly cut it and I need a change. I go along to the Vidal Sassoon training school, which costs £10. I take a magazine photo of the Elnett hairspray advertisement and tell the trainee hairdresser that it's that hairstyle I want – all bouffant, loose curls and just lovely. It's been washed and now Mary the hairdresser starts to cut, but she's cutting it really very short just above my ear.

"Are you sure you're not cutting it a little too short?" I ask, showing her the picture again. She says nothing and on she goes and I'm now worried because an awful lot of hair has come from the back of my head. I ask her to get the manager, who comes over and literally gasps. It's all too late. You can't put hair back that's been cut and I look like a boy but, interestingly, I get quite a few compliments. I stop crying and wonder if I was crying for the loss of Jon or for my hair.

I rent a new flat in Highbury, which was originally a large house now divided into four. God, I feel so lucky that I found it. My flat is on the ground floor and the sitting room must have originally been a rather grand hall or dining room. It's been divided up to create a second bedroom and you can tell because the partition is flimsy. There's a massive marble fireplace with a mantelpiece that I can barely reach and floor to ceiling windows looking out to the wide, tree-lined road. It's fully furnished with a tiny internal windowless kitchen just beyond my bedroom. At the end of the hallway there's a bathroom with a back door leading to the large shared garden. Upstairs live the Shearers, an elderly retired couple. Next door to me is a constant change of tenants, mostly Aussies, and in the basement is Marjorie, also old.

My first flatmate is Caroley. She and I work at the same company, Charles Barker, where I'm PA to the chief exec and she's PA to the MD. She's only recently joined and is frightfully glamorous, resembling a young Elizabeth Taylor with huge hair and rosebud lips. It's the mid-70s now and these are heady days. Her huge hair is augmented with a hairpiece and I discovered she stuffs scarves down her bra to make her boobs appear bigger. These scarves have a habit of disengaging from her bra and sliding out the bottom of her dress. Luckily this mostly happens in the flat, meaning I come across snakes of scarves all over the floor. Caroley oozes sex appeal and manages to attract the opposite sex in droves, so you can imagine my shock when I walk into her bedroom one morning and discover the MD in bed with her. Bloody hell!

A regular haunt is the La Valbonne nightclub in Kingly Street, near Regent Street. I don't know how she does it, what with work and always so busy and then off out all the time. Maybe I'm jealous? The only men I attract are half my size with pot bellies. She reminds me of a rather exotic Turkish belly dancer. I am horrified when I catch her shaving her upper lip.

"What are you doing, Caroley? For God's sake, you'll end up

with a thick moustache!"

"Who cares?" she says. "I'll worry about that when I'm older."

I'm footloose and fancy-free and I'm having a fine time, despite the pot-bellied men I seem to attract.

***

My friend Sarah has invited me to supper (supper is usually one course whereas if you're invited out to dinner, that's three) at her frightfully poncey Cadogan Square flat. This is not your average, bog-standard flat or the kind of ones I inhabit. This place is simply stunning with enormous rooms and floor to ceiling windows that Sarah's parents bought for her to share with her two younger siblings. She says she wants to introduce me to a male friend of hers because she reckons we'll get on, and you know what? We do.

Her friend makes me laugh and he has a slightly effeminate way about him and so, a new relationship begins. He's called Jon, too, so that's fortunate. Well, it's Jonathan really and he has a two-up two-down cottage in Cookham Dean and I'm now in my furnished rented flat in Highbury. Jonathan is a sound recordist for the BBC and later will set up his own company. He's a workaholic; always busy.

About this time, my old friend Caroline – or Caro – who was at school with me in Darjeeling and again at PNEU, moves in to my flat because she's split up with her long-term boyfriend and has nowhere to live. We've known each other since we were six. I can't stand her ex-boyfriend and hope they've split up for good.

In 1976, I start work at Charles Barker, the biggest advertising agency in the world at that time and who'd just made the world's most expensive advertisement for Chanel where a beautiful model floats through an actual bottle of Chanel. This is the best of jobs. I'm PA/ secretary to Reg Valin, managing director of their City subsidiary that specialises in financial communications. They produce exciting stuff called tombstone advertising and design annual reports and accounts for banks and insurance companies. I don't have a clue about the advertising world and I struggle with the relaxed attitude. Everyone is called by their first name but I can't seem to call my boss by his. I find it difficult having come from a culture of seriousness, manual typewriters, telex machines and Colonel Roper. That aside, I love the job and the advertising world and it's just down the road from Fleet Street, which is always abuzz. We're not far from St Paul's Cathedral and Mother Bunches wine bar, too. Avery's, down some stone steps just off Fleet Street, has a straightforward menu consisting of three main meals, which come in large shallow containers. There is usually a large meat pie, a lasagne, a vegetarian option and a counter with different salads. It's always busy and my go-to place for lunch.

This is the job where I learn to create lists, my to-do lists, and everyone is light and easy and good fun. I morph into this hip person. Everything was so full-on in the 1970s and yet it was simpler – or perhaps seemed simpler because I was younger. You are such a different person, too, in your 20s, which is the age I am in the 1970s. A mad, bad time but so much fun also. It was a time of unthinking, of careering around, always in a rush and lots and lots of lines of coke, blues and pinks. Anything that speeds me up, I'm up for.

I'd always been too scared to try cocaine, coke or Charlie. Jax was really into it; actually, she was into everything and I thought she was dead cool. Your 20s are a tricky age. Appearance is so important and for me it was all about 'achieving' success, making money, always 'doing' and never 'being'. 'Being' was for those hippy, new age 'om' meditating-type people who didn't have a proper job and who had loads of time on their hands – or so I thought.

Jax is beautiful with a stunning figure to boot. Every boy is attracted to her and her teeth are straight. I am envious of her teeth. She has the most stunning smile and there is something otherworldly about her. It seemed she simply floated on a cloud; nothing really bothered her. She loved everyone and looked like a Pre-Raphaelite goddess. I, too, have a good figure – shame about my nose – but in every other way I was the opposite of Jax. I want to get somewhere. I don't want to drift. I've also got a proper job whereas my Sussex gang are laid-back. That's great when I'm there for the weekend but not so good when I need to be back in London bright and cheery on a Monday. Those little blue pills help.

When I tried coke for the first time Jax was going out with Gary. You could say Gary was the boyfriend from hell. We used to call him 'Squeaky Wallet' because he'd rarely open it to pay for a drink but was very good-looking and had a certain boyish charm. We were on a barge in the Kew part of London when Gary brought out this all white powder, all new to me.

"What's that?" I asked.

"Well, see what you think, Penskew. But take it easy as this stuff's really expensive."

I was nervous of getting it wrong and scared of the reaction I'd get if I took it. Instead of sniffing, I snorted – out – and white powder went flying everywhere. "Sorry; oh God, sorry," I said.

"It's okay, I suppose. Here, try again."

I did and after a while it's a lovely feeling. I am wide awake and I so need to be wide awake sometimes.

With the second Jon now off the scene, a man called Charles sends me poetry and love notes in his seduction of me. I'm flattered and end up at his flat with its silver glittery wallpaper and mirrors. I am shocked at the gaudiness considering his father owns a bank. We have sex and play mah-jongg but, apparently, I'm not playing according to the rules –*his* rules. We argue, he gets stroppy and brattish and the next morning he drops me off at Hyde Park Corner, which is nowhere near Farringdon Street where I need to be. He takes off in his car and I wonder how the hell I'm going to get to bloody work.

After two years at the company I'm in my early 20s and Reg turns 40. I buy him a chocolate birthday cake but forget to put the bases under the candles, so wax spills all over the chocolate icing and it's inedible.

Chapter Fourteen

Turning 21 and a New Job

My 21st was a rather splendid affair, which I shared with Jax. We hired Plumpton Racecourse because you could in those days. There was a ton of booze and I think there were nibbly bits, probably cheese and pineapple on sticks, cocktail sausages and crisps – lots of crisps. We drank from plastic beakers, a lot of which ended up on the race track; it was a drag (literally!) the next day having to find these strays when we returned for the clear-up. Everyone was smoking. Mine were the heavy-duty Marlboro Reds variety.

I get a pure silver engraved hairbrush set, with comb and mirror, and money from Mummy and Daddy. The money pays for the party. Gaga sends me a red plastic weekend valise suitcase, which is thrown out immediately. I receive a plastic, turquoise bead necklace from Auntie Biddy and throw this out, too. Not totally successful on the present front then.

I am called into the boss' office when it is explained to me that Reg Valin and Richard Pollen plan on leaving Charles Barker to set up a new company and they ask if I would like to go too. Yes, please! I love my job and working for Reg Valin and am really pleased and honoured they think I'm good enough. For the next three months we do our usual work at Charles Barker and then at the end of the day we drive to Southampton Row where the Valin Pollen office is to be set up. The plan is to be officially open on Columbus Day in October. Mailing letters are sent out and we get our first client, a merchant Irish bank called Guinness Mahon. We hire a girl called Sarah through a recruitment agency to be PA to Richard Pollen.

Reg and Richard have offices next to each other while Sarah and I share. It makes me mad that she always leaves early on a Friday for Shabbat. I can never leave early, not that I particularly want to. Anyway, apart from that Sarah is really fun and on April Fools' Day we put cling film on the men's urinals and buy magic soap that turns hands blue. Soon, though, the offices are too small as we're growing at quite an alarming rate.

We move just around the corner to Bedford Row where we've soon got departments like a Creative Department, an Accounts Department and Account Executives. I'm getting more responsibility, too, and just down the road you can buy these fabulous egg, avocado and bacon sandwiches. I also acquire my first company car, a VW Golf, and buy my flat. Both my flatmates Caroline, and then Sue, were articled clerks training to be solicitors, having studied law at university. What I didn't know then, but realise now, was that in their legal training and eagerness they managed to find a loophole in my tenancy agreement and with that I became a sitting tenant, which meant the landlord wouldn't be able to get me out easily if he wished and had to give me the chance to buy the flat, which I managed to do for a song. Even so, it's still a struggle to find a deposit and I'm fed up of living in sub-zero temperatures with Calor Gas burners. My number one priority is to put in central heating. I also need a stereo system and Robert at work comes with me because I don't have a clue and I buy a Sony record player. My first album is Engelbert Humperdinck's 'Release Me'. I'm really trendy (not) and perhaps it's an omen because Jonathan then releases *me*; well, he found someone else and split up with me. I reckon it went back to that time we stayed at the Holiday Inn or it could have been the Hilton in Birmingham. We came back from a meal out and, while I was violently sick in the loo, the loo seat crashes onto my nose, leaving two bumps and a bruise. Not a good look.

It's 1985 and Valin Pollen keeps on growing so now we've moved to Grosvenor Gardens. I've been there – well, I was a founding member, actually – since 1979. I love my job; I love everything about it. I love the long hours, the fact that I can drive to work and park easily. I love the social life – just everything. I have a great company car – this is my second and it's a Panther Kallister, green with gold swirls all over it, and it's won some design award for its, err… design. I'm really proud of it.

My days consist of working hard, going home to my flat in Highbury and driving down to Sussex to stay with my best friend at weekends. It's a whole world away from my London life. I usually drive down after the pubs shut at around 11pm on Friday when there's hardly any traffic and I cruise with the roof down, feeling pleased. I have already had a couple of glasses of wine, but so what? These are the days when everyone drinks, everyone smokes and we're always at the pub in the evening. Thursdays are the best as there's only Friday of the working week left and a hangover on a Friday is cope-able.

I recall a time when I went round Trafalgar Square twice trying to find the way home but hey, so what? When Friday comes around I'm cruising down to Sussex. I must remember to drink some milk to line my stomach because I haven't eaten anything and Jax and Manda don't cook unless it's a roast on a Sunday – they do a mean roast chicken. Once, the leftover carcass was put back in the oven and forgotten about. When that oven was opened a couple of weeks later, the carcass was some sort of animal that had a fur body again and could almost walk out on its own.

Again, I live in two completely different worlds. During the working week I am the serious admin person, tip-tap-typing away, interviewing potential secretaries who have to endure the blue atmosphere of my smoke-filled office. Come Friday night I drive down to see my 'real' friends and am introduced to their world of dope. Although I don't smoke dope as it just puts me to sleep, I'm into coke and the multicoloured speed pills of which my favourite are blues. With this, it means I can go to bed at five in the morning on a Monday and still get up to drive back to London to be at my desk for eight, feeling really alive and thoroughly alert. Yaay, I've found the answer to being able to party endlessly and still manage my job!

Valin Pollen is now really big and I run a department of 17 people. I've got a deputy, Fiona, who's brilliant and we've just taken on a new internal messenger boy called Julian who is a six feet eight athlete and towers above all of us. His job is to distribute all the internal memos, meeting notes, anything really that needs to be taken from one department – this is before e-mail – to another. We now occupy most of the buildings in Grosvenor Gardens and so there's a lot of running about involved and he's perfect for the job.

Lovely David shows Julian the ropes, but after a few days I start getting calls from various secretaries saying, 'he's a bit scary', 'he looks at me funny' or 'I find him really intimidating'. *Uh-oh.*

My department is very friendly and we work great as a team together with maintenance guys, messengers, secretaries and spare secretaries in case a department needs extra. Julian doesn't join in though, and is moody and sulky. Right, that's it; he'll have to go. Because he is so big and bulky though, I decide to call in a couple of other male directors to support me. Here goes. So, I start off, 'Julian, I know you've only been with us a week or so and, although there have been no complaints about the actual delivery of mail, unfortunately a number of secretaries are finding you a little intimidating'.

My partition wall is smashed down in one bang with his arm. Next, it's my four-drawer metal filing cabinet, which concertinas inward. With the two directors edging towards the door and me stuck behind my desk, I realise that if he chooses to attack me, I don't stand a chance. Luckily, my lot have been briefed that if they ever hear something odd from my office, to call the police. They duly arrive, but his rampage doesn't end as he continues to break desks and chairs and generally becomes animal-like. These were the days when, unless a person has personally been harmed, the police would not get involved. It was a frightening event and continued to be scary because the next day I had his girlfriend on the phone denying Julian would ever do anything like that and demanding he get his job back. By this time, too, I'm driving my gorgeous soft-top Panther Kallister and terrified that he'll find it and me and smash the roof in on me.

***

I once had a boyfriend called Kevin whose name my poor mother couldn't accept. 'Kevin? Oh no, darling, that name will never do. We'll call him Paul'.

I met Kevin at a party and I didn't want to take him seriously as he was a permanent student – in other words, had no money, and look at me; I'm a hotshot in advertising! He also occasionally wore eyeliner and went around in fatigues and bare feet, but holy shit was he a master in bed! The thing is, he didn't care what anyone thought about him and so when it came to introducing him to my parents and he turned up shoeless, I knew things were not going to go well. He lived in Brighton and I always referred to him as my 'toy boy' even though we were the same age. I forgave him a lot, especially the time he pulled me by my hair from out of The Hurlingham Club after a VP summer party in front of EVERYONE. He also wrote off my Panther car after I'd not had it long, but when I found out he was stringing me along with someone called Tracy (I ask you!) Well! I should give credit where credit is due, however. He installed a whole new kitchen in my flat as well as a loft space, so I thank him for that.

***

I bite my thumbs... the skin, really. I pick, pick, pick, peeling the skin back and when I can get a big enough hold, I bite it off. I'm a cannibal. It's a disgusting habit but I can't help myself. It's become such a habit that I don't know I'm doing it and these days the biting usually takes place whilst driving. Maybe it started as a nervous thing, to replace Boneys, which I gave up when I was 14. I wasn't one of those people who automatically stuck their thumb in their mouth during the day. I only ever sucked my thumb with Boneys at night, under the covers. I'm not interested in biting my nails, which was why I had to give up sucking my thumb. The nail got too long and cut into my gum.

The skin picking and chewing is so therapeutic, except of course it isn't. Quite often the thumbs bleed and get quite sore and so I try to smooth the sores, but when the scabs arrive I pick at them again. Kevin advised shaving the edges of the thumbs and actually that helped for a while; my thumbs lost their scabby lumpiness.

Chapter Fifteen

Jerome

And there he was, with hair just curling over his collar, a lovely moustache and his green-grey eyes so sad. As soon as I saw him for the first time in the North Star pub that Saturday night, the bar littered with lines of coke, I knew that this was the man for me or maybe I thought he looked the steady type who wouldn't mess me around like the others had. I think I was attracted to his brown corduroy trousers first. They were so comforting to look at. Those loose-fitting trousers, those soulful eyes, but he was also incredibly thin. He came over as a gentleman, like my father – a gentle man.

I find out he's half Belgian but why that has anything to do with anything, I've no idea. A girl had just left on the back of some guy's motorbike when Mick, the pub owner and friend of mine said, 'Hey! Come over and meet a new addition to the village', quietly adding, 'I don't think he's that happy, Penskew, but I think you'll like him'.

Over the course of the evening I discovered that the girl on the back of the bike was the man's wife. She returned later looking dishevelled and this delicious-looking man left sheepishly to have 'dinner with my wife'. After all those lines of coke, too. I wasn't hungry.

It was a gentle introduction and we meet at the pub on the weekends I'm down, which is basically every weekend. We slowly get to know each other and he makes me laugh. When he tells me the story of how he and his wife went to New York for his job and how, a few weeks later, she left a note in their flat telling him she'd gone back to England, maybe I should have thought a bit...

He works in IT for American Express and has a small terraced cottage in a village about a 20-minute drive out of Brighton. I still have my Highbury flat. Most of the time he drives up to London and we go out for dinner. At weekends I drive down to stay in his cottage.

***

It's the night before my wedding and I'm terrified and excited at the same time. I'm staying at my parents' flat, which tradition dictates but, surprisingly, my parents didn't really want me to. 'Wouldn't you rather stay in your own flat, darling?' they asked. When I think back to how traditional my parents were, I'm amazed and a little upset that they didn't automatically assume I would stay with them.

My mother is a little 'orf' because she wants me to have my hair done, but of course I ignored that. Hate having my hair done anyway. For years my mother has announced to me, 'Your hair's a mess. You really must wear lipstick, darling. Your face looks completely drained otherwise'.

To me, this is her way of telling me that I'm ugly, but no request for organising this wedding is too much trouble. In fact, my mother is in her element in the organising of everything. She clearly thinks I'm not a very organised person and can't possibly organise my own wedding even though I'm head of administration and personnel and extremely organised and efficient! I'm now quite senior at VP but my mother still feels I should be told how to be and how to dress. She's remarkable, really.

Jax by now is living in Florida but happens to be over at this time. She's my best woman and is coming up with Manda and a few others from Sussex. The ceremony is taking place at Kensington and Chelsea Register Office because I can't marry in a church as Jerome has been married before and I don't go to church. Neither do I live in Chelsea. I've had to borrow a friend's Chelsea address and I'm actually a little scared that I will be required to write this down. I do all I can to commit it to memory. Right from the start my married life begins with a lie.

Despite all this, I'm so happy and feel that this is it for me. The reception is being held at the fabulous Oriental Club just off Oxford Street where Daddy's a member.

The register office service (or should I say wedding) is booked for 10am and when I look out of the window I can see the weather is rather iffy, gloomy even, and it looks like it might rain. It's August for goodness sake but feels more like March. My bed for the one night in my parents' flat is a most uncomfortable camp bed with metal legs and a canvas base, but it doesn't really matter, as sleep is the last thing on my mind.

When morning comes, I dress carefully in the long, white, satin affair that my father and I chose together in Selfridges – or it might have been Peter Jones. Nothing 'designer' about it but it is pretty, fits me like a glove and shows off my figure. Jerome, together with his best man, have stayed the night in my flat in Highbury, which I guess is why I so wanted to stay at my parents' place – I definitely would not have wanted Jerome to see my wedding outfit before we got to the register office. The deal is we'll arrive separately.

Daddy has booked a chauffeur-driven Daimler for our transport to the register office and we leave the flat at 9am, which means we arrive at least half an hour too early and have to drive around the block several times. I feel really embarrassed because I assume everyone – that is every person wandering the streets – somehow knows that this idiot of a bride has arrived ridiculously early for her wedding. I may be efficient and organised but perhaps a little too much on this occasion!

After a register office ceremony, which just involved a couple of close friends and immediate family on both sides, we progress to the reception venue. At the Oriental Club there's a sweeping staircase and chandeliers and in the garden a marquee has been erected – all for me! I think I've around 150 people coming including everyone from my department at VP. The film department are also there, recording for posterity.

Jerome, Daddy and I stand to greet guests as they arrive. There's Geraldine, one of our two receptionists, clearly pissed. She walks over gingerly and I feel deeply sorry that she is in this state. I've known for a while that she's been drinking on reception during the day at work. I learn this when I find her litre bottle of white wine hidden under the counter, but I'm just keeping an eye on the situation because she still answers the phone okay and puts callers through to the right people. Her partner on reception, Jan, is regularly beaten up by her partner. It's all a bit of a mess and I need to sort it out, but I feel so sorry for both of them and losing their jobs won't help.

The formal reception with the finger food, delicate sandwiches, cocktail sausages and canapés, is not due to start until 3pm so there are a couple of hours to kill. Daddy has organised for the immediate families – my parents, my horrid aunt, Jerome's parents, his three siblings and Jax – to have lunch in one of the rooms of the Oriental Club. I've been allocated a separate room to change into my going-away outfit, except I'm not actually going anywhere yet but back to my flat before catching our flight to Spain the next day.

My mother is like a little bird, flitting in and out. I notice she doesn't look her usual immaculate self. Maybe it's the colour of the clothes she's wearing – grey, which drains the colour from her face. Her hair isn't done, not in its usual hairsprayed splendour. She's organised all this, sent out the invitations, compiled the wedding list, sorted my flowers, the cake – everything – and all within my parents' annual leave of six weeks. So perhaps she's just nervous or, more likely, stressed.

After lunch, Jax and I go off into my changing room and chop up a couple of lines of coke ahead of the reception. You know, just to keep us going.

The best man did go on and on about rings never ending – that is, the never-ending circle of a wedding band/ring which relates to the circle of life and that a marriage is everlasting, as well as about tribes in East Africa (or something). His speech contains nothing personal about Jerome and I, but then again, he doesn't know us well and I don't know why Jerome chose him as best man.

At last it's over and I'm trying to hide the fact that I'm smoking because it really doesn't look that cool puffing away in a white wedding dress. With the lines of coke I need to smoke, though – it always makes me want to smoke. I go over to my father to say thank you for everything and he replies, 'I'll send the bill to Seville', which is where I'm headed for my honeymoon. He *is* funny.

I've organised another party in the evening back at my North London flat, which also has a marquee in the garden. This was a bit of a mistake because the reception was at 3pm and my evening do isn't until 8pm, by which time people will have either become so drunk on Champagne or fallen asleep in the gap in-between; by the evening they wouldn't have enough energy to be going out yet again. So it was a quiet affair.

Chapter Sixteen

Being 30 and Married

I loved my 30s. Well, actually, I loved being 30 and loved it when my first daughter was born at 32, but I could have done without my 40s altogether.

***

I'm married now and trying to get used to saying, 'My husband...' I thought that once I'd got married my life would be more like my parents had, except I'm not sure I was thinking at all. In a nutshell, I'm married, it's 1986 and my mother is ecstatic. He's not quite top-drawer of course and he's not a duke or an earl, but he's not called Kevin either (what a blessing) and to my mother's eyes all is as it should be.

I'm in love but I'm not sure what I was looking for in a marriage. I think I was looking for security, mainly – for love, for the safety of being in a partnership of mutual supportiveness and for fun and friendship. Having had a couple of serious relationships that I thought would end in marriage, I was relieved to be settling into some sort of marital bliss. I had a great job, great money and those first two years of marriage could be described as idyllic. Oh, okay, I mean, I *did* get a little peed off when each morning I would catch the train up to London Victoria at 7.32, arriving home 12 hours later to find that Jerome had been home for hours, sunning himself in the garden. I think I probably did occasionally say something; I was good at sarcasm. We were always having people round or going to friends' houses, so life was full-on and I didn't dwell on it – after all, Jerome only worked down the road in Brighton, so it wasn't so surprising that he didn't need to leave before me and would get home earlier.

Commuting drained my energy, but on the way home there was

a buffet car where you could buy cheese on toast. I'd have that along with a couple of gin and tonics. I once fell asleep and ended up in Portsmouth. That was annoying, but at least I wasn't drinking in the morning unlike the men I saw ordering shots of whiskey first thing. They were probably journalists.

Our married life in those early days was crazy. There were crowds of us. Life was one big swirl of parties, smoking joints, lots and lots of drinking and lines of coke.

I met Jane at around the same time I met Jerome. She worked in the North Star pub where we regularly gathered. Jane was part of the crowd with her boyfriend, Phil. She knew Jerome before I came along and when she married Phil in 1985 we became a close friendship foursome.

We were at Phil and Jane's once and Jerome was wearing a flowing Nehru coat with pantaloon trousers and those gold slippers with the turned-up toes that he'd bought on a recent trip to Pakistan. Suddenly there was a crash outside. Some poor guy had come off his bike. When Jerome and Phil went out to help and the guy looked up at them from the ditch he was lying in, he must have wondered if he'd died and gone to heaven.

We found our house shortly after we got married. Some of it is over 400 years old and started life as two cottages. It has a huge lounge with French glass doors on two sides, which is great for parties and best of all is the swimming pool. It even has a sauna. The downside is that it's right on the A23 on the way to Brighton, which, at the height of summer, gets busy. If you sit at the top of the swimming pool slide you can wave at all the traffic queuing towards the coast. Now, of course, they've extended the A23 and the pool has been filled in.

A very ornate spiral staircase in a smaller sitting room winds up to bedrooms and bathrooms and up further to a tiny wee door, like a fairy door that you have to bend down to get through. There's another narrow staircase to two attic rooms. It's not your bog-standard house. I loved it and would definitely say that I was so much more enthusiastic about it than Jerome. It sat at the very top end of our budget, which, at the time we bought it in 1986 was £150,000.

It has lots of nooks and crannies and some of the rooms scare me, especially the attic. Also, the big sitting room has curtains that I need to draw shut every evening because there are so many windows for whomever – mainly spooks – to look in. It *is* an eerie house but as soon as I had my daughter, H, to look after all my silly irrational fears, the feeling subsided. I knew I would protect her no matter what.

In these early years Jerome was away a lot and, one evening, when I was pottering in the kitchen in the dark, I looked up and there, with his bearded face pressed right up against the kitchen window, was a bloke. *Jeez!* I actually did think it was Jesus Christ for a second. All he wanted were directions to the squat that had been set up over the other side of the dual carriageway. They often had a bonfire going and people dancing around. Another time, a huge stretch limo turned up and this dishevelled bloke and his friends came knocking, asking if they could look around. He'd apparently grown up in the house and remembered he'd had a swing in the downstairs spare bedroom. Finally, there was a time when I swore I heard the French doors slide open, but it was nothing.

***

It's October 1987 and, as usual, I get up in the dark and go downstairs to make a cup of tea, but there's no power. Thinking there must've been a power cut, I decide to drive to the station and head for work. As I get to the car I look around and wonder briefly why there are huge piles of leaves on the ground, but nevertheless I get in my soft-top Panther Kallister. Of course, I'm not going anywhere. There are fallen tree trunks all over the place. I return home, ring work and open the sitting room curtains. *Bloody hell!* The Indian bean tree in the middle of the garden is lying on its side right up against the French windows, there are fences down and everywhere is a huge mess. What happened? I turn on the radio and all becomes clear. There's been a hurricane and I didn't hear a bloody thing!

This time was a kind of magic in a way. It was three days before power was restored. We lit lots of candles, I'd cook roast lamb and potatoes in our inglenook fireplace and there was a certain silence around.

Chapter Seventeen

Kashmir and my Mother

I left VP in early 1988 for no other reason except I was bored. Bored with the commuting. Just plain bored and tired from my 12-hour days. I wanted to do something more meaningful, which is a joke, as I didn't get to be meaningful for a very long time. In fact, for a long while my life became fairly meaningless. Jerome got a job in Johannesburg earning good money, certainly more than he would earn if he carried on working here. The day I decided to resign from my job, I think this absolutely terrified Jerome, as I was the bigger earner. Communication, though, was not our forte and Jerome, in any event, always had a hankering to live and work abroad. I found this exciting, actually – new horizons, new opportunities. This all came about whilst I was working out my three-month notice. I left at the end of March 1988 and Jerome's new IT job in South Africa started in May, with a trip to India squeezed in in April.

We started off thinking that we'd rent our house out, but that idea came to an end when some senior army chap arrived to look around it for an Arab family who were interested. He said that he'd had problems finding properties for Arab families to rent as they quite liked to light fires in the middle of rooms for the purpose of cooking. So that put paid to that! In the end my sister-in-law Maria, who was a nurse, took a job at a Sussex hospital and we suggested she might like to live in our house while we were away.

So, we headed to India to see my parents. My father booked us a houseboat on Nigeen Lake in Kashmir – such a treat, as, although I'd been before, this was a first for Jerome. The whole holiday was 10 days, a couple of days in Delhi followed by a long weekend in Kashmir, then back to Delhi to catch an onward flight to Calcutta for a further few days before flying back to the UK.

The houseboats are arranged side by side but not so close that you can jump from one to another. There would be boat 'taxis' that collect you from your houseboat and drop you off on the edge of town, which in this case was the capital, Srinagar. We'd visit the buzzing market, fighting our way through the masses of people in tiny, narrow streets with stalls either side. Staying on a houseboat was incredibly peaceful. In the evening we'd play cards – no TV.

Although we expect my parents to visit while we're in South Africa, we don't intend to holiday in India again until our two years is up. South Africa, we have been told so often, is a world within a country and there is just so much to do and see that there really wouldn't be the time.

I know that something is not right when mother is not at the airport to meet us. She has never, in all the years I have been travelling back and forth, ever missed my arrival. Instead, my father is there, all six feet four of him with a rather large girth from the giving up of smoking following my mother's second bout of cancer.

"Where's Mummy?" I ask.

"Oh, nothing to worry about. She's hurt her shoulder. She's back at the apartment, excited to see you."

Okayee. We arrive but there's no sign of Mummy.

"Hellooooo?" I call. This is just not like her. I knock on her bedroom door and am shocked and totally flabbergasted at the sight of my mother, usually always immaculate but now shabby-looking, makeup-less and stooped over with messy hair. I can't believe it. *This is my mother?* It suddenly strikes me that this is what my parents do – make it all up, make it look good for their one and only, always treating me like a child. I am never a grown-up in their eyes because they've never confided in me and therefore have always treated me as this child who's got to be protected from everything. The paradox is that, ostensibly, they happily sent me to boarding school a whole day and night's train journey away up a bloody mountain at the age of five, and then at eight over to England to boarding school. They were totally complicit in creating this completely independent person who had to fend for herself from a young age, but have never really recognised me as a grown-up.

My father is utterly clueless about my mother, his wife.

"We can't go to Kashmir and stay on a houseboat," I say. "We must get home to Calcutta to get Mummy to a hospital; she's really ill."

"Nonsense, we are going to Kashmir and that's it. As I said, she's just strained her shoulder. She'll be fine in the mountain air."

I could go on and on with the detail of it all, about how crazy it was, but the point is we *did* go to Kashmir – and I'm ashamed to say that now. I did not fight with my father. I always did what I was told. Not that it would have made a difference. It would not have changed his mind even if I had. I doubt, too, Jerome felt he was in a position to intervene.

Our houseboat is called Serenity. All the houseboats that lie side by side have wonderful names – Sunshine, Butterfly, Peacock and Crystal Palace. They are phenomenal with intricately carved walnut panels that divide up the rooms and wooden ceilings – all with detailed carving. It is stunning and in every room there is a wood-burning stove situated right in the middle with its chimney flue stretching up through the ceiling. Indian rugs cover the floors.

Kashmir and Nigeen Lake are the most magical of places and, after Phulbari, is possibly my most favourite place in the whole world. The houseboat has a covered veranda at the lakeside with steps that go down into the lake itself. Behind the veranda is a sitting room with comfy sofas, coffee tables and tables for playing cards, which backs onto the small dining room. The scent from all the walnut panels is gorgeous. A passageway runs from the dining area past what is my parents' bedroom, then the bathroom, then mine and my husband's bedroom with its own bathroom.

But during the long weekend on Nigeen Lake, I feel really low. I'm not happy about Mummy. She's getting weaker and is not really able to walk unless I hold her upright. I can tell she's in a lot of pain but she hardly says anything at all. She can't eat by herself so the bearers or myself help. Within a couple of days, she can't stand up at all. Something is very wrong and I tell Daddy that we must get a doctor. It is impossible to get through to my father but at long last I manage to ask him to bring a local doctor.

The sight of my mother shocks him as I try to give him some of her medical history.

"She had a mastectomy in the early 70s, followed by a

hysterectomy. She fell over a rug a couple of years ago and broke her wrist. Now, I don't know what's wrong but my father says she's got a sore shoulder. I think it's more than that."

"Well, Mrs Penny, I think you are correct. Your mother is very seriously ill and needs hospitalisation as soon as possible. When are you leaving Kashmir?"

"Not till the day after tomorrow."

"May I suggest, Mrs Penny, that this departure is of the utmost importance. Madame here has broken a lot of bones – her ribs – and is why she cannot contain her body any longer. She is unable, ma'am, to stand upright in herself."

Oh, shiiiiiiit!

"How will I get her to Calcutta?" I ask.

"Well, ma'am, it will be difficult, sincerely difficult."

About bloody right. I'm playing cards with Daddy and my husband and I relay all that the doctor has said, but still my father completely ignores me. I seethe in silence as my completely detached father continues his game. Maybe it's a man thing this emotionless persona, this thinking that everything's going to be okay.

"Shall we go up to Gulmarg tomorrow?" my father suggests.

Oh, so it's just going to be another ordinary day? I don't want to leave my mother but grumpily agree a change of scene would be good. Gulmarg has the highest golf course in the world and we toboggan in the snow and behave as if everything is normal.

My mother, oh my mother. Back on the houseboat I tuck her up with a blanket on the veranda's wooden seat. Kashmir is high and it is chilly, but the view is simply stunning. The lake, which in reality is probably filthy, shimmers in the early morning, a soft mist lying low above. It is truly sensational. Early morning brings Mr Bul-bul, the flower man, on his shikhara – his boat that is covered in beautiful blooms. It glides up to the steps of each houseboat.

"Eh, you want bul-bul flowers? You want?" he shouts. The fruit man and the cigarette wallah follow him.

The mountains are before us with their sprinkling of snow and, honestly, you could quite believe you were in Xanadu – except for my mother. We had a terrible time trying to get back to Calcutta. Wheelchairs at that time in Kashmir were not readily available and our flights were from Srinagar to Delhi and then on to Calcutta – journeys of around six hours each all told. Our driver Mohammed greets us at DumDum Airport and we drive as swiftly as possible, which isn't swiftly at all in the heaving streets of Calcutta, to the Woodlands Nursing Home. It is in actual fact the hospital where I had my tonsils out all those years ago.

I honestly don't recall Jerome offering me any support at all during this torrid time or even that I asked for it. My concern was all-consuming for my mother's welfare and I didn't pay any attention to Jerome. All I remember is feeling terribly distracted and depressed and not knowing who to turn to for it all to be better, for all the bad stuff with my mother to go away. By the time we get back to Calcutta, there are only two or three days left before we return to the UK.

Is my father taking anything on board? Is anyone there? I am not hopeful about my mother's outcome. At this point she has 'gone'. There is no possibility of a sensible conversation. She makes no sense of anything. She constantly wants to go to the loo but just when we get there, with me holding her up because she can no longer put weight on her legs, she doesn't want to anymore and cries to go back to bed. What with the puja festivals happening at the time, it wasn't possible to get the proper medication and testing kits to see what was actually wrong with my mother.

By this time I know I've lost her. Her mind is frazzled, she can't remember stuff and all she really wants to do is write lists. Lists have been her life – a list for the cook for the week's meals and a list for Krishna, our head bearer. Lovely, gentle Krishna, for whom nothing was too much trouble. He adored my mother and in her own way I think she adored him back.

So, she's writing these lists for Krishna who is ever present, standing beside her hospital bed after rushing to her side once we'd got to Calcutta. She gives him endless notes about what has to be done that day, a list for her volunteering work, a list for the cook and a list for Krishna himself. Her lists, though, are gobbledygook; no words, just lots of lines and she doesn't make any sense when she tries to talk. She is not in her right mind, but she seems happy. My father plays bridge with her, possibly a little one-sided.

The thing is, or rather what *I* think it is, is when you are so proper, as my mother thought she was – *so* proper in her thinking, *so* rigid in the words she used: 'It's not 'OFF', Penny, it's 'ORF'!' I feel that perhaps it's that rigidity of the mind that can't hold up the body properly anymore, so her bones get eaten away and, in the end, her hatred of un-properness made her body disintegrate.

She died of cancer of the bone marrow in simplistic terms, but on her death certificate her cause of death is 'Cardio-respiratory failure in a case of multiple myeloma complicated with septicaemia and renal failure'. If we'd gone to Calcutta rather than Kashmir, we could have possibly found out what was wrong, but it would still have been too late to do anything.

My father would not allow me to stay for her final few days – 'your duty is to be beside your husband', he had said. I miserably left on the Wednesday, feeling terribly sad and as if I were swimming in treacle. I gave her a peck on the cheek but she no longer knew me. Days later I was on my way back after receiving the news of her death.

Chapter Eighteen

Secrets

Being in India, she was fully made up in the funeral home with a thick powder base, bright blue eye shadow, bright pink cheeks and bright orange lipstick. She did not look like my mother at all. As I looked at her lying in her open casket, I thought it was strange to be visiting a funeral parlour, which, to all intents and purposes, resembled an ordinary house.

There seemed to be many women crouched on their haunches just keeping guard, as it were, over her casket. I also remember that the Indian way is to never allow the mourner to be left by themselves – just like my father wasn't – until I arrived back in the country. I didn't cry at seeing her because the person lying there did not look like the mother I remembered and with so many people around I felt embarrassed. My father had already told me he'd done with his crying and from that first evening of my arrival there would be no more tears from him, not that I'd seen him crying anyway.

The funeral was an immense affair, crowds of people, or so it seemed to me as I looked out under my foggy tears. All of Calcutta had come out to mourn and pay their respects to Sheilah Gertrude Rome – she hated the Gertrude bit so that was not included on her gravestone. It was a boiling hot day and I was wearing dark blue. I had sweat pouring ('not sweat, darling, it's perspiration') down my body and tears pouring down my face.

After the funeral, I went through my mother's things. Oh blimey, what a state. There were hundreds of old newspapers stuffed into cupboards and clothes not neatly stacked. No wonder my father kept his things in a separate room. I had no idea. The bearers came in and asked if they could have some items of hers for what I presume were sentimental purposes. 'Of course', I said, 'Please, help yourself', and they do. The strange thing is, these two men take mainly her bras –

one side of which is padded because she'd had a mastectomy. They take a couple of blouses and a silk scarf, too. I honestly didn't take much notice but because the bras were such odd things to choose, I do remember that.

Her stuff was in such a mess – crammed full in cupboards, all topsy-turvy – that there was nothing I particularly cared about except for a heavily beaded black jacket that I remember we bought together in Delhi a few years earlier – I still have it today.

While occupied with the post-funeral events, I was thinking of Jerome already in South Africa. I felt guilty about not being there with him, confused and worried that I was letting him down. I really just wanted to get the whole thing over with and get going to South Africa.

Finally, I come to my mother's four-drawer filing cabinet and start sifting through the mess of paperwork and wow! What the hell? There are photos of Sheilah as a baby and I can't work out why it says the date that it does on the reverse of every photo: 'Sheilah in her pram, 1917' and 'Sheilah, aged 2, 1919' when I know perfectly well she was born in 1927. That's the date on her passport and on every other piece of legal documentation I've come across over all the years prior to this moment. Imagine… this forlorn four-drawer filing cabinet with its lies inside has been here all this time. For goodness sake, 1927 is on her gravestone – engraved forever.

This is where I find out her date of birth is actually 1917, not 1927 as I believed, and she had a half-sister, Frances. I rush through to where my father is sitting reading the newspaper. I tell him of my discovery and ask if he knew? 'Of course', he replies, chuckling. 'No-one else in the family knows, though, but I doctored her passport to make her my age'. I'm sure this is illegal – oh well.

Damn, I wish I'd asked my mother more questions or that she had told me more, but she was a keeper of secrets. I wish there was a dial-up code to wherever she is so that I can ask her for answers to the questions I have. Actually, she didn't really have secrets, she just never talked about her early life – absolutely nothing – to the point that, when she died, I discovered she was actually 11 years older than my father and that she had a half-sister who was 18 years older than she was. Her sister, Frances, died two years after I was born so I'll never know why there was so much animosity, but I had, however, read solicitor's letters saying how little my mother wanted to know about her half-sister. Eighteen years is a lifetime's age gap.

When I found all this out, my imagination fired up and various members of my family – mainly my father and Aunt Biddy – started giving me titbits of information. Had I heard, for instance, that my mother's parents died in a road traffic accident down in Kotagiri? Or that Frances was a product of an encounter with a local woman because of my mother's mother spending so much time in England? Or that my grandfather actually had two houses in Kotagiri, one for the family and one for his mistress who'd had his child, Frances?

It turns out none of that is remotely true and the story is rather more sad and mundane. My mother's father, Francis, had been married before to Elizabeth De La Nougerede and that marriage produced their daughter, Frances. Unhelpfully, the British Library records her surname as Lanongerede and if you Google that, you only get two results. She tragically died young, aged 34, of pneumonia, leaving her small daughter, Frances, behind. Frances was sent to England to live with her father's sister in Hampstead before being sent to St Margaret's Convent School and Orphanage in East Grinstead. Her father then met my maternal grandmother, Gertrude May Goodall, who was one of eight children. They were married on 31st October 1906 and had my mother 11 years later. I do wonder what happened during those 11 years of no children. My mother's parents' entire working lives were in what is now Pakistan and then India. Her father was in Customs in Karachi, which is where my mother was born in 1917.

On my mother's side, they all died young. My mother was only 69 and her sister, Frances, only 58 when she passed away in Brighton, just six miles from where I live today. The house in Burgess Hill is even closer and, even though I spent over 10 years living and working in London, my strange family circle is almost closed. On my father's side, even though they originally hailed from Liverpool, his mother and sister ended up in a small village between Worthing and Burgess Hill.

When her father died in 1931 in Burgess Hill, my mother was not at his bedside. Instead, his first-born daughter was, as was his wife, my mother's mother. It seems extraordinary that my mother wasn't there, too, when she was literally a 10-minute walk away at the Parents' National Educational Union (PNEU). I suppose she was only 14 and, perhaps because she was a minor, her name wasn't recorded on his death certificate or maybe she was considered too young to be at her father's deathbed.

When I used to think about my mother's early life it would make me sad, but in actual fact her life would have been similar to those Raj days. She, too, was sent away to a boarding school, just not at such a young age as I. My father said he regretted sending me to boarding school at five years old and my mother had said it was to get me used to boarding in England. When I think back now to that time, I spent so many hours crying while packing, driving to the airport and waiting in the departure lounge. I feel exhausted just thinking about it.

In those days – and in my day, too – children were sent to boarding school in England from a very young age and did not return to India for long periods of time. Back in the 30s and 40s it was quite normal for the wives of that time to return to England and be there for the duration of the children's education. The husbands would continue to do their work in India and their wives would rent or buy a house near to where their child was schooling. Therefore, husbands and fathers were left to their own devices while their wives were absent.

My mother was educated at PNEU Burgess Hill, West Sussex, the same school I attended many years later, a girls' day and boarding school set up specifically for children whose parents lived abroad. Throughout her schooling, my mother didn't see her parents for seven years. During those seven years, in fact, throughout her entire education, she was fostered out to another family during the holidays.

Chapter Nineteen

South Africa

After my mother's funeral, I flew back to England to repack and join Jerome in Johannesburg. It was during the apartheid era and some of our friends didn't think we should go to a country like that. I am too naïve to understand why.

After a few weeks of settling in, we move out of the house in Hillsborough we shared with one of Jerome's work colleagues and move to a posher area called Illovo where we rent a townhouse. Jerome has bought an old Mercedes and, once parked in the garage, there are seven locks to master and open just to get into the house, plus an internal metal gate separating the ground floor from the first. These were precautions against potential intruders who were inclined to be violent (even though we were in a sought-after area). All sorts of nastiness was going on in Johannesburg at that time, although nothing compared to what I believe it is like now.

I feel like I'm camping or on holiday. I just can't imagine living here for the next two years. I don't have any of my usual bits and pieces around me and feel all discombobulated. After the trauma of my mother's death, the rush back to India for her funeral, returning to the UK and then, days later, heading to South Africa, I hadn't given enough attention to what I needed in order to feel at home in Johannesburg.

I have an old school friend living in Johannesburg and I spend time with her, but there's only so much tennis one can play. This is home for my friend, but I certainly don't feel at home and am still trying to find my way around. I do manage to get the house furnished, albeit sparsely.

It's a Saturday and, for some reason, Jerome and I end up attending a talk on Persian and Oriental carpets given by a Victor Lidchi. He is a well-known and respected dealer in Jo'burg, although I didn't know it at the time. It turns out he's looking for a secretary-cum-dogsbody and offers me a job which is where I meet Suzi, a white Afrikaans lady who does Victor's books. My job 'ees to creeate leests of all the rugs available for sale bicos ivery month Victor holds a sale een a hotel, sometimes in Jo'burg, but more often out een the steecks in very Afrikaans areas. Of course, they often happen at weekends which ees kind of restreecting as that's when Jerome is free'.

Suzi and I become really good friends but I don't like the way she treats her black cleaner who she makes run after her car when she's supposed to be giving her a lift home. She thinks this is funny and it's not. I say nothing, not wanting to get on the wrong side of Suzi because we have to share an office and work closely together. Although Suzi is much older than me, she is fun and full of energy. She introduces us to lots of her friends and so a social life begins.

There was that drunken evening of which I have no memory – well, what I mean is, I remember everything up to a certain point and then it's just blank. When I wake up the next morning in our super king-size bed, I am right over one side and Jerome is way over the other and I feel a nasty, cold shiver go up my spine.

"What is it?" I ask.

Silence.

"Oh, come on, why are you way over there? What's going on?"

"You don't remember, do you?"

Remember? "Well, I know I was drunk but so were you. It was a great evening, wasn't it? Great dancing; I mean, I don't exactly remember going to bed, but hey–"

"You told me you hated me. You slapped me across my face."

What? "Don't be crazy," I say. "I don't do things like that. I love you."

I am frightened by his coldness and I begin to beg. But no, he is a granite rock, immovable and black. When he's gone to work, I sit and think. I'm very ashamed but I still cannot believe what he tells me I've done. I ring two of my closest friends and sob and cry and say that I know I drink too much on occasions, but I have never hit anyone or abused anyone whilst drunk. I'm the one that makes the drunken phone calls at two in the morning and will use baby talk or just fall asleep. I do not hit.

My best friends agree. I look at my hand, the one that is supposed to have hit him, and I don't see any marks or feel any tingling. Surely there would be something there to confirm what I did? Surely? This creates the teeniest bit of distance between him and I.

Due to complications with Jerome's company's tax situation and fears that it could turn violent, we stayed in South Africa for just one year instead of two as planned. The first and only Christmas we have in Johannesburg, we are invited to spend it with some friends in the Kruger National Park. Someone's parents owned a property on the edge of a dried-up riverbed. There is no electricity and running water is debatable. I didn't realise it was going to be *so* basic but it was all a big adventure to me. Basically, no-one dares move in the 40°C heat so we spend a lot of the day lying on our makeshift beds on the veranda drinking dry martinis – not exactly cooling! Our view of the desert is immense and an occasional elephant wanders by.

There's a higher than usual watch tower nearby, which I assume is used by tourists and safari guides to track for animals. The view from its summit is stunning. It's so high that there's a cool-ish breeze up there but the midges bite us to pieces and down below are the ominous growls of lions – any animal sounds seemed like they were immediately below our tower, but in actual fact were quite far away. Still, I was terrified but Jerome never showed fear; it's like he just didn't seem to care if we got attacked by a wild animal or not. He was always calm in any crisis whereas I was a bunch of nerves and hysterical. Christmas dinner was a laugh with us all dressed up – boys in bow ties, boxer shorts and shirtless, girls in long evening dresses. It was difficult to know what we were eating as most of it was covered in flies. The only way to deal with this was to get blotto.

***

By the New Year of 1989, I had to get back to Calcutta to help my father pack as he was retiring. My parents had previously bought a flat in Victoria, London, in readiness for retirement, although they had had a couple of flats before this one, one of them being in Paddington – 'no, darling, Bayswater!' My father was someone who didn't hold onto things and I was worried he'd throw things out that held fond memories for me, particularly if they were to do with my mother. I book flights via Kenya and it's a relief to be out of Johannesburg and back home with familiar smells and familiar people.

When my father retired, he was the only white person permanently employed in the tea company in Calcutta, which by this time had been taken over by the Khaitan family. Back in 1949, he was one of many white people – well, more than many since it was very much a British company with British managing staff in all its offices – on all its tea plantations and factories throughout India and further afield to Kenya. After retiring, my father was offered a job at the London office. That didn't last long. I don't think he could bear to be part of a team when he'd been *someone* in the Calcutta office – like when he was at the Oriental Club he was *someone* there too.

In some ways, my mother's death in 1988 turned out to be a good thing. She wouldn't have coped very well. What would she have done with no good works to get involved with? In Calcutta, my parents had status. Basically, she was stuck in the days of the Raj, a queen of all she surveyed. I wonder, too, where my mother thought home was. She'd spent pretty much the whole of her life in India. The only time she was away was the nine years she was educated in England when travel was perhaps too expensive or too slow to make going home for the holidays a possibility. She then spent two of those nine years at Charlotte Mason College training to be a teacher before a stint at the Royal Academy of Music. All her other learning, her secretarial skills, were done in Delhi. I come across a scrappy piece of tracing paper among her files and in every single exam she takes she comes out with a Distinction or a First-Class Diploma. She had so much potential.

Now that I'm looking back on my life, I realise my mother never had any close girlfriends. I don't recall her laughing or giggling hysterically with a group of girlfriends. It was all bridge mornings and mahjong afternoons, bridge evenings, dinner parties and stiff upper lips.

Chapter Twenty

Becoming a Mother

I didn't give mothering much thought before I became a mother. Come to think of it, I hadn't given much thought to being married, either. Considering that I was an only child and that most of my early years were at a boarding school, I hadn't had any experience of, well, anything. Becoming a mother came as a shock. First of all, you fall in love with your child and then it's the ceaseless getting up in the night and the constant chasing of sleep. I really thought (except I didn't really think) that it would be a huge doddle. After all, I'd had years of working long, long hours and I'd run a department of 17. How difficult can being a mother to one tiny baby really be? Eh?

My father's reaction to me being pregnant was rather lukewarm but I put that down to the fact that my mother had died the year before and he'd just returned to England to retire.

I don't recall Jerome being particularly overjoyed, as he doesn't really have big, emotional outpourings for *any* reason. I remember those nine months as nine months of being huge; I enjoyed being able to eat what I liked but perhaps should have been more thoughtful about this. When I had my first cup of tea in the morning, I would raid the biscuit box and take a couple of chocolate digestives. *Good for you,* I tell myself, *give yourself a pat on the back; you're getting nothing from anyone else round here.* I found cutting out the booze pretty easy really and I cut down on the smoking, too, down to about three a day. Jane was pregnant with her second child by this time, too.

So, I've got the baby and I am so happy about this new beginning in my married life. It means we are now a family and it makes me feel warm and goosepimply when I think how great it is all going to be. I am besotted with my child and I'm also completely neurotic. My world has turned upside down. I don't want to party, I don't want to go out, I don't want anyone around, I just want to nest with our baby and for the three of us to be together to enjoy every moment.

Unfortunately, I seem to be the only person overjoyed about this massive event. Poor H has got colic and starts crying round about 6pm and doesn't let up for a minute. Jerome is great at first and spends ages rocking her and walking round and round the pool table trying to get H to calm down.

I don't work – or rather, what I mean is I don't work full time. I want to be home with H. I do bits that I get paid for but I'll never be able to earn like I did before and wouldn't want to. These days, or rather, back then I used to be embarrassed about my housewife/ mother status, but being a mother is the most important job in the world and, now when I look back, I do hope I've done a good job of it. There's been many a time in social situations when a typical question was, 'So, what do you do?' and I mumble shamefacedly that I am *just* a housewife and mother.

Having been an only child and never having been around any other children, I now have one of my own and I'm in a muddle. I know she needs feeding except I did forget to do that in the hospital. Well, I didn't think you had to if she didn't cry, so how was I supposed to know? She got jaundice so we had to stay in longer. I know she needs to be clean and I know I love her. It's more than simple love, it is all-consuming. I'm just exhausted, breastfeeding, trying the manual pump (hopeless) and I'm up all night long. I'm dog-tired, I need help and am not getting any but I don't ask for help either; I'm hell-bent on doing everything by myself because I think it's expected. Jerome goes out to work and I'm the homemaker. The trouble, too, is that Jerome is away for work a lot – it's either Pakistan, San Francisco or Yemen – and when he's back it's only for a couple of nights before he's off again and he's knackered, too.

How can you be a good mother when you don't have a mother yourself when you're growing up? It is so difficult being a mother having not been surrounded by a family who loved you, who showed affection and emotion and said things like 'I love you'. I had no nurturing to speak of. I have my gorgeous daughter who I am besotted with but she's a baby and I need to be giving her my full attention 24-7 – no let-up. I am wound up like a ball of string but this ball of string is stuck together and is not unwindable. I take it all very seriously. I cannot relax for a minute.

My oldest was born feisty just like I remember my mother was. She was no pushover, but I just believed all children did as they were told by their parents and always behaved well, so it was a shock when my oldest didn't. I couldn't understand why she was constantly egging me, pushing my limits. Not that I had a limit. I gave in to her all the time and I cried a lot knowing that I wasn't doing either of us any good. She was perfectly wonderful when we visited friends and when she went on play dates, but when it was just her and I, I found it endlessly boring. H would have seen me cry on numerous occasions. I was full of fear and loathing of myself. I had no-one setting me an example, no-one to relate to or show me what to do.

I struggled with motherhood and the huge responsibility of it all. I was not an easy-going mother and I was definitely not a natural earth mother/ maternal type. One day when H was a baby, I heard someone on the radio say their favourite day of the week was a Sunday when they could lounge around in bed and spread the newspapers all over it to read at their leisure. It was a bliss that I could no longer imagine. A lie-in on a Sunday was a pipe dream – and someone else's.

In my desperation I start to pray again. I used to, at my mother's suggestion, say prayers kneeling beside my bed when I was little. My praying now is a cry for help. 'Please God, help me; please let H not wake up so I can sleep longer', but then I would think what that might mean for H not to wake up at all and she might die in the night, so then I start to panic and pray some more… 'Please God, help me…' I often pray while sitting on the loo because it's the only time I know I will be on my own. I'm so tired knowing I need to be up at 5am when my child wakes up.

At the rare times Jerome is actually home in Sussex, he is often in the pub and then off to our closest friends' house of Phil and Jane, smoking the wacky baccy and quaffing red wine. At weekends he's in bed feigning sleep. I'm so confused with the lack of any emotional connection from my supposed husband and other half.

Of course, the reasons I was always pretty manic was because I was always trying to do several things at the same time and not asking for help: trying to get a meal organised, putting H to bed, breastfeeding for 11 months and counting down to the next fag. There's a party going on in our house every Saturday night and I really, really want to join in ad I'm getting irritable with H, wondering why she won't bloody well go to sleep which, of course, upsets her and keeps her even more wide awake. Instead, I get cross, mostly with myself, and cry upstairs. I resent that he is able to enjoy himself at our party with the music turned up loud when I'm upstairs trying to put the little one to bed all by myself. 'Sweetie, please could you turn the music down?'

I got so hung up about everything back then. I was impatience personified, dealing with life at full speed without giving the meaning of life any thought at all. It was all such a damn rush – manic – but I just had to get it all done. That goes back to my busy working life at Valin Pollen. When I became a full-time mother, I brought it home. I didn't know what was happening to me. I was always so independent. I could cope with everything, but since I'd given birth my whole world had fallen apart and my marriage was pretty ropey, too. I was constantly tired and was doing everything all by myself.

Chapter Twenty-One

Anguish, Slowness and Mess

I'm a nervous wreck because H and I are flying to Florida to stay with Jax. I have visited many times before, but this is the first time I'm travelling with an 18-month-old on my own. Frankly, I'm terrified. How the hell am I going to cope with a tantrum on a flight that can take anything up to 10 hours? *Eeek.* I have packed a carry-on bag, which I have filled with lots and lots of 'doing' things: stickers (she loves stickers), reading books, colouring books, colouring pens, Play-Doh, Plasticine, cars and building bricks. You see? I'm prepared practically but not emotionally. I'm also feeling low, a gloominess which seems to be constant in my life at this time. I just can't cheer up so a trip to see my best friend is going to be the thing. Jerome can't cope with me when I'm like this so getting away is good.

It was during that holiday I began to realise I wasn't quite right in the head. H and I share a double bed but I'm not waking up until 10.30am, but when I *do* wake up I am full of dread for the day ahead. How will I fill it? What do I do to entertain my child? There is darkness and the time goes ever so s-l-o-w-l-y. I didn't understand that when you're in something called depression, you don't know you have had it until you come out the other side.

I didn't have a car in Florida and even if I had, I'm not sure I would have been capable of driving and on the wrong side of the road, too. Jax was at work a lot so I couldn't easily go anywhere, which was why it was such a blessing to meet her next-door neighbour, Nancy. So, H and I would walk down to the lake where there were signs saying 'Beware of Alligators' and we'd sit on the sandy edge playing. What was I thinking? Why did I do this? I can't imagine. Obviously, we didn't get eaten, but Jee-zus!

Feeding H was hard. The food was unfamiliar to her and baked beans on toast was about all I could manage. Poor Jax hadn't got a clue what to do. She was busy in her full-time job arriving home in time to see me feeding H baked beans *again*. She got quite cross with me. She's pretty cross with me now, generally, but at this stage she hadn't got children yet, so she didn't understand.

Soon I am saved by Nancy. She lives in one of the oldest houses in Delray Beach. It's a very friendly neighbourhood and over the many years of visiting I've come to know quite a few people there. Nancy was married to Charles and it seemed weird that an American could be called Charles. To me, it is an English name. He wasn't a Chas either and he ate with his mouth open, smacking his lips like a fish. Nancy and Charles had two boys, the youngest just a bit younger than H. For the life of me I can't remember how we first met but H and I spent a lot of time over at her house, H playing with Nancy's youngest. Nancy would take us out for fun lunches in restaurants geared for kids that had things for them to play on. It was just such a relief to find someone like-minded.

Jax has a heart of gold but her timekeeping is not. She has a problem with time and motion. In other words, she is always bloody late for everything. She tries to cram too much into her day and ends up not getting everything done, which usually involves letting someone down. She has to make her bed before she leaves for work, which she does studiously by stripping it right back and making sure the bottom sheet is flat even though she's already running late. She does the strangest things, like, if she is due to meet someone at, say, 4pm, she'll decide to have a shower – 'won't take two seconds' – at 3.58pm! Her time, then, is inclined to work backwards.

She was supposed to be meeting H and I at Miami International Airport for this, our first visit, and if you've never been to Miami airport, I will tell you that there is nothing to do there, especially for an 18-month-old. It takes hours to get through Immigration, the security staff are menacing and not at all helpful. I try to phone (this is before mobile phones) but I need a quarter for the phone box, which I don't have. I don't know how to reverse charges in America and I have a very fractious, tired child. Two hours later, she arrives. When I reminded Jax of this a short while ago she'd forgotten, but we can laugh about it now. In fact, she and I simply have to look at each other and we fall about in hysterics. If she says she's 'just nipping to the shops' or 'won't be 10 minutes', invariably it's more like an hour. I honestly don't know how she copes with it or how she manages her life. The times we've all hung around waiting for Jax to get ready to go out for breakfast and end up going out for lunch...

Jax is also very, very funny. My girls adore her and she is godmother to the oldest, H. She can't see properly, either. It's getting better although the eye she's had fixed is red in the middle, strangely, like there's a warning light off in the distance. It's rather like seeing one of those red flashing lights you get on a buoy that's bouncing out at sea, except now she has a cataract in the other non-flashing eye that, according to the optician in Florida, is so big that if it's not dealt with in the next couple of months she'll go blind. Once, when we were all piled in her car, my girls, Jax and I, Jax saw what she thought was a dog on a lead. My oldest piped up, 'Well, you get a lot of those at the airport, Jax', because what she actually saw was one of those pullalong suitcases. Still cracks me up now. On shopping trips she has been known to have two different shoes on.

Jax never does anything she says she'll do. For instance, she'll say, 'I'll ring you next Saturday', but never does. Christmas and birthday cards are several days late. When it comes to gift giving, she quite obviously forgets what she's given you – I have three pairs of very similar earrings, which she has given me over the years. I realise that she's a bit thoughtless, which I think is due to her trying to do too much at the same time. There have been many times when I could have done with her support, but I don't think she is capable of offering any because she can barely cope with herself. I think it's because she lacked the maternal love of her mother who died young. Although her big sister was always there and did the best she could, that sister was only 16 when the girls' parents died. Jax was 11 and her big sister 15 when their father died and their mother died a year later. Her sister was a teenager trying to deal with tragic loss and a younger sibling at the same time.

That Florida holiday did cheer me up, though, mainly because of Nancy and her kids and just being in the sun and heat. A few years later we fly out again, but this time the three of us, for a family holiday. The day before we're due to fly, H falls down the back stairs with scissors in her hand and stabs herself just above the eye. You should have seen the blood. I was completely hopeless, in a total panic, but luckily Jerome was a rock in situations like this and we rushed H to the doctor. Butterfly plasters were stuck on but her face was a mess, all swollen, with massive black eyes. You can imagine the looks we got as we boarded the plane.

Jerome lightens up a lot when he's on holiday and, as long as we're doing things that he's interested in, all is okay. We had a lot of fun between the four of us – Jax and her husband Chris, Jerome and I. There is a lot of laughter, easy banter and glasses of wine. H is brilliant with her bedtime routine and will be ready for bed at 7pm after a story, which is when I feel able to relax and chill.

***

The bottom line is, I'm a mess. I resent this parenting business, a business you can't resign from, and I always think I'm missing out. Sometimes when I'm sitting quietly in the dark, when it is night, the rain is lashing against the window panes and the wind is howling, I find myself returning to Phulbari with how easy, lovely and simple my life was back then.

There's so much stuff going on inside my head that it's easier for me to think it is my fault. I am home alone, yet again with the baby. I don't mind because I don't want to go out in the evening because it's such a hassle taking the baby, too, plus I'm breastfeeding, not drinking and I just can't relax. Jerome doesn't like me bringing the baby into the warmth of the marital bed so I end up sitting in the cane rocking chair in the baby's room, which is two rooms away, in the dark and in the cold. I don't like that my precious child is only a few months old and has been relegated to her cot two rooms away. Will I hear her cry? He says the baby keeps him awake when she cries and that he has to go to work in the morning.

I breastfeed in the dark space. I rock the chair hoping that a rocking movement and a breast will surely rock my child to sleep, and occasionally it does. Then I hear the knocking. *What's that?* Click, click, tap, tap, tap. *Oh, what's that?* Is someone trying to get my attention? I'm scared. Before I know it, I let my imagination run away with me and on the opposite wall of my rocking chair I've created a whole scene. It's all a bit bloody spooky in my old house as I sit and watch unfold before me what I have created. There are people and trees and horses and camels and bushes all moving. They're going someplace along a desert landscape, but I don't know where. Even though I'm not really religious it feels religious somehow. *Trees and bushes don't move, silly,* I say to myself, but they move in the wind of my imagination, back and forth. *Is it the wind that moves our thoughts?*

It's not all bad. It's 1991 and I've made friends with a group of girls who all have toddlers H's age. We met at a mother and toddler group and regularly get together for lunch and for the children to play in one or other of our houses. Pauline has Jessica, Hazel has Ryan – the only boy – and Mitzi has Nicole. It's so lovely and our chance to relax a bit. There are toddler groups in the afternoons and slowly I'm beginning to feel back to myself a bit.

Part Two
Middlings and Musings

Chapter Twenty-One

Diary

H is two and I find the diary Jane has given me and start writing:

***

It all boils down to the fact that now we've got our first born, Jerome has gone down in the pecking order. He's only down to No2 and I've dropped to No3 or even No4 if his mother is staying with us. No2 is not good enough, he wants to be No1. Oh God, it's so difficult. He just goes into a mood, won't speak about or engage in conversation. He takes himself off and becomes remote.

***

1994 was a terrible year. I am ashamed to say that I was banned for drink-driving. I reckon my real slide into misery started here. Lots of badness happened in 1994 – it was stupid to leave Jane's house and drive home when I'd had too much to drink and when there was a major police TV advertising and poster campaign about drink-driving at that time. Three police cars stopped me. When I look back at diaries from that time, they make very hard reading. I mention that I am drinking on every single page. I am drowning in alcohol and am clearly lost. I'm okay during the day but come the evening when H has gone to sleep and I'm downstairs on my own, I start to drink. Jerome drinks with me when he's around.

He was supportive enough after my arrest. He came with me to court, but there was no affection, no putting his arm around me saying, 'Don't worry, Penwen, we'll get through this together'.

***

H and I didn't see a lot of my father. I think H was terrified of him because he was huge in height and girth and he never came down to her level to play. Mind you, if he had he wouldn't have been able to get back up again. He didn't smile much either, so to a little girl he must have been quite scary. Also, I was terrified of any possible bad behaviour on H's part in front of him. Once H became older he was a lot better. He didn't go out of his way to put us at ease in his presence in his flat, though. There was one jigsaw puzzle that got made each time we visited although we did go to the zoo on a couple of occasions. He just wasn't grandfather material, really; didn't know what to do, so emotionally he was always detached but was very generous when it came to helping me financially.

***

Without a driving licence, I now need to rely on friends and neighbours to drive H and I to school and pick her up later. I want to be there because I can't bear the idea of a relative stranger meeting her in the school playground. Jerome has bought me a bike and has attached an electronic thing called a ZETA machine to the back of it. This powers the bike – you see, he's good like that – but it still doesn't go fast and all the rushing that is part of my life, that I have become so good at, comes to a crashing halt. It now takes ages to get anywhere and I really have to plan every day very carefully. Cycling to the nearest shop is a two- to three-hour round trip and involves a steep climb up a hill, the same hill where I got stopped and breathalysed.

***

I need Jerome, but so, it seems, does our friend Jane. She is becoming quite dependent on him, needing his help for various things, more than usual. Her husband, Phil, works in London. Twice now within a week Jane has asked for help which involves Jerome going over there and now she's calling again: 'Is there anyone around who can drive me down to Brighton for my works' do?' She must mean Jerome as no-one else around here can drive. This causes major rows between Jerome and I. I am gobsmacked at how quickly he jumps to respond to Jane's demands! It's astounding. No doubt you can see where this is going, even if I couldn't at the time.

***

Whenever Jerome and Jane get together (which is pretty much every single night when he'll 'drop' round to hers after work or the pub), I imagine they talk about high-minded stuff, but what exactly *is* that? I think they gang up on me. I wonder, too, if someone tipped off the police on that dreadful night when I was stopped for drink-driving.

Ever since I got my licence back, I never get into a car even after just one glass of wine. Lesson learnt.

Chapter Twenty-Three

Delray Beach, Florida

I am so looking forward to this holiday even though H and I have already been out earlier in the year. I'm looking forward to everything – the plane journey, being able to drive the hire car (since I'm still banned in England), arriving at Jax's, opening pressies, H going to bed very well as always that first night (and every night, frankly) and Jax and I staying up not too late drinking and me smoking.

After that first night, Jerome starts to read a book Jax has given him and that's it. Bang goes the family part of the holiday. Luckily, I love playing with H at the beach but a teeny-weeny part of me would also like to have a moment to be able to read a book myself and I find it extraordinary that Jerome is able to concentrate to the extent that absolutely nothing – least of all his daughter – matters. So, the holiday is not quite how I imagined it would be.

At the end of the holiday, Jax suggests that she and I should go shopping and leave H with Jerome for once. I ask her to ask him and she is shocked at his response: 'I hadn't anticipated this and it's really not a good idea'.

On another occasion on that hols, Jax suggested that Jerome take H to the park to give me a break and I was so grateful. They were back within 10 minutes. Whoopie!

***

I've been keeping diaries for three years now and don't leave them lying around. I carefully hide them behind my mirrored clothes cupboard and stack them neatly behind the difficult-to-reach-behind chest of drawers, but somehow Jerome found them although I didn't know this until I was rereading one a couple of years later and discovered he'd written comments in the margin like 'This is a load of crap' or 'You can't say things like this' and 'God, it's like you're talking to another person'.

Well, it was exactly that because I had no-one else to speak to! I couldn't talk to Jane because I didn't trust her not to tell Jerome.

***

I can't find my plastic bag of love letters from Jon, my first love, from all those years ago and I blame Jerome for this. We never discussed them or the diaries as by the time I discovered his notes in my diaries and the missing letters, we were almost on the point of officially separating. I did ask about my love letters, but I never got to the bottom of what happened to them, sadly, as they were wonderful.

***

We've booked an Easter holiday to Kenya, very expensive, and I'm so looking forward to heat. H, aged seven, is doubtful about the whole thing mainly because of injections. Jerome and I have bickered most of the day before, although I don't think H has noticed particularly except she's not been in a good mood herself, anyway. Perhaps sullen is a better description. Basically, I was not in a good place or state and this must have rubbed off on H. I hate myself and hate that I felt overpowered by Jerome. I feel inferior, unworthy, useless. It's hard to read my diaries from this time and I think I made a total hash-up with H, poor girl.

***

It's been a pretty dreadful week and it all started because he, as was his wont, gave us the usual five-second warning about us all sitting down round the table to eat our supper. That would have been fine, but I'd already said H could eat her meal in front of the TV because she'd asked earlier. But, no. Jerome comes striding in turning off the TV, telling H to move to the dining room. He never does anything nicely and consequently she bursts into tears and goes upstairs. All this happens whilst I'm serving up the hot food, but I know that during the time I take to go upstairs to comfort H, my plate of food will go cold.

H comes down after our chat and together we eat in front of the TV, which I turn back on. By this time Jerome is mad, really mad. He announces that he's cancelled our Kenya holiday and after we've had our injections done, too.

The Kenya holiday wasn't cancelled, he was bluffing. He then apologised for his momentary madness. Is the memory of anything bad supposed to disappear? I have my diary.

***

At this point, Jerome hadn't had a full-time job for seven months and wants me to get a paid job. I'm not sure how I'm supposed to do that when I already have a full-time job at home because he does nothing to help around the house.

I have been told over the years by various friends that I should be grateful to the now ex-husband because he took us on many wonderful holidays and indeed he did, but what's the point of these wonderful times when there's no affection involved, no friendship, no support and, ultimately, no love?

Kenya was a prime example – Diani Beach, our room almost on the beach itself, with an awesome view right out to sea. The enormous night sky was filled with stars, wonderful when romance is in the air, but it wasn't. We went for a 10-day break. Lunch and dinner are served beneath a thatched canopy. It was glorious and H and I played in the sand, not just building castles but digging down to create a whole town with tunnels and bridges.

Jerome and I are not getting on and he spends his evenings at a nightclub while H and I go to the hotel bar and restaurant. It's brilliant because there's a really good-looking guy behind the bar doing magic tricks for all the children. H loves this and I love him. I'm so desperate for affection. A couple of days later I'm lounging on a sunbed just outside our hut; I've slathered suntan lotion all over me and have my hair tied back. I really look a mess when who should come sauntering by but the good-looking magician. His name is Michael and he asks if I'd like to go for a walk. I most certainly do. Jerome and H have gone for a walk in the other direction. One thing leads to another, but mostly I enjoy our chats. He comes up to see me every evening once H is in bed and Jerome is wherever he is and, during the day, we meet in his room and on the beach and swim in the sea. I can see Jerome wandering up the beach and I can't believe he doesn't notice Michael and I walking hand in hand only a few feet away. All this time I have felt such an ugly person, but Michael makes me feel beautiful and special and because he spends lots of time with me, surely I can't be such a bad person after all?

***

Back home, I'm on cloud nine and imagining a whole other life. I imagine Michael phoning or e-mailing me, saying that he can't live without me even though we only knew each other for seven days, if that. It didn't occur to me that he saw me as some lonely idiot woman whose husband took no notice of her. Easy prey. I don't know what to do or how to be or even how to think, except I'm not thinking. I am trying to be kind to Jerome, but I cannot continue to live my life without love or affection.

It's such an effort to get up each morning and be cheerful for my daughter's sake. Jerome cranks up the music, so there's no possibility of conversation, only turning it down in the early hours of the morning.

***

I went down to Brighton to meet my father and I told him everything. He was so supportive and understanding, calling Jerome 'a boor', but he doesn't want to know the details.

***

Jerome has cottoned on that something is amiss when I tell him about Michael a few months after our return. It's piqued his interest and suddenly he starts to open up about himself and us. 'Look', he says, 'let's make more of a go; I'll try harder', but I think I've already tried very hard and every time I get a metaphorical slap in the face.

He's including me in this making-a-go-of-things when I don't feel I'm at fault, but now he's coming over as really genuine and maybe our lousy relationship might improve. So, we try and our relationship *does* get better and before I know where I am, I'm pregnant. We were in a good place, so it was a pleasure to find out I was going to have a baby, as I'd always wanted a second child. This time I felt it would be a boy. Good times, lots to celebrate. The only blot came from my father who was shocked about it, having heard a lot of my sob stories. He was confused, which made me feel bad.

***

H was coming up to nine when her sister P was born. It never occurred to me that Jerome would go back to his nasty ways after P was born but, sadly, it took no time at all. It was a huge blessing having Jerome's mother Jose around, known as Nana, since she was now living with us while waiting for a place in sheltered accommodation. She helped enormously and I was a lot more relaxed second time around, too.

It's a new beginning, except it's not all sunshine and roses because H has problems adapting to having to share her father and I with a baby that requires all my attention. She's struggling and there are problems at school, too. H wants to be with me on her own. She doesn't want P anywhere near me and will creep onto the sofa to snuggle with me even though I'm feeding P. It's difficult.

With Jose now moved in and my joy at providing H with a sister, I bought an enormous super king-size bed so that I could keep the baby in her Moses basket at the end of it. The bed was big enough that any movement on my part wouldn't bother Jerome.

Having the new baby and with our relationship on a bit of an even keel again, life was rolling along nicely. Trouble started when my awful aunt, Biddy, got cross with me for breastfeeding my fractious, crying baby at the back of the church during her ex-husband's funeral. It was either that or let the baby squeal and interrupt the service.

***

P has definitely started saying whole words now. She's 13 months old. She calls me 'Maba', 'Hada' for H and 'Teetee' for Easter (that's the cat). She says 'bye bye' very nicely and waves – waves at everyone and says 'hewo' for 'Hello' and to everybody, too. It's 'teeda' for thank you and 'do-doo to be co-coo' for 'can you put the animal DVD on the computer?' It's a scream, as is she.

***

Now two years after P was born, I don't understand why J is being so horrid. There have been so many moments now of horridness that they've overtaken the times that have been fun. I am treading carefully – on eggshells – in case I say something that will upset him.

I mustn't – repeat – mustn't say anything about his father. I mustn't, even about the time when his father was leaning over our first-born with a cigarette dangling precariously out of his wet-whisky-laden lips, the ash about to fall on my daughter's upturned, beautiful, shining face.

At Christmas the girls are not allowed to open their Christmas stockings until Jerome has got up and, bearing in mind the girls are excited and are wide awake at 5am, it's mean of him to expect them to wait until he emerges at 9ish.

The mending of our marriage didn't last long as you can't repair a marriage unless both parties are prepared to put in the effort, but we did see in the new millennium brilliantly with friends with a bonfire and fireworks. Because I wanted to, I woke P up and brought her out wrapped up in a blanket. She won't remember, of course, but hopefully H does.

***

I'm being called all sorts of nasty names but the one that really gets me is when he says 'You're drunk' when I've only had a couple of glasses of wine; however, since I *do* have a couple of glasses most evenings, I am now beginning to wonder if I have a drink problem and he's right and I'm all wrong. Yes, that must be it. There are times when I don't remember stuff and I'm on edge all the time, can't relax at all, need to be alert. I'm in deep trouble and struggling with the stress of it all. I have a very lively two-year-old. I have bad circulation in my toes. I have a constant upset tummy, which I have had for at least a year, possibly longer. Every other day I get the runs and I need to get to a loo immediately; it really is touch and go. I'm feeling unbelievably anxious and stressed. I'm tense all the time and those glasses of wine in the evening send me over the edge and, most frustratingly of all, I don't remember the next day. During my working days in London there was a lot of drinking and smoking and it was fun. It's not fun anymore and I'm not sure my body can cope with it now and, as usual, I am doing everything on my own.

There was a time when getting an upset tummy was heaven because it meant you would lose weight and you could get into those jeans a couple of sizes too small that you'd bought. You'd lie on the bed to squeeze in your stomach, hold your breath and pull the sodding zip together. Alternatively, if the jeans were too big it was a case of getting into a bath full of water in order to shrink them to fit. For some reason my jeans always had a huge gap at the waist where my back met my bum, which was annoying.

***

I pray a lot and I'm so glad I've got my own thoughts and that Jerome can't see inside my head. This is what I say to myself when I'm praying in the family bathroom upstairs. I pray for help but I also have hateful thoughts about Jerome and I'm pleased he can't tell.

***

You may remember I mentioned Manda earlier. She is Jax's older sister by four years and is remarkable in lots of ways. You will recall she was only 15 when their father died, and a year later their mother, so although I consider Manda a friend, she has this air of maturity and responsibility because she was forced to take charge of her younger sister when she should have been out enjoying her teenage years. It's why I think of her more as a surrogate mother instead of a friend.

***

Manda is a most wonderful friend and is able to see exactly how things are with me. She talks so much sense and just yesterday when I was miserable, thinking I was an alcoholic, she managed to see through everything. In basically one sentence, which is unusual for her, she said, 'Penskew, you are absolutely fine and, yes, occasionally you can drink too much but you are definitely not an alcoholic'. It made me feel so much better that I'm not a bad person after all. I enjoy a drink and that's all there is to it. I go one night without a drink and keep a list of how much I *do* drink. I also try to stop smoking. I mustn't say 'giving up' because according to the book *The Easy Way to Stop Smoking*, which I read cover to cover, says 'giving up' sounds like you're giving up something enjoyable and it's not... except it is.

***

I've got to try to make sense of my marital crisis. I'm in such a muddle and so incapable of dealing with this. All I want is love and support. I decide I need to find a counsellor. My friend is seeing a psychotherapist because she's in crisis with her marriage break-up, so I decide to give him a go. My first visit begins with me lying down on a couch. After the second session he sends me home with homework and asks me to write a fairy story, which I thought was a bit much when I'm paying him a small fortune.

So, I write:

'Once upon a time there were two fairies – a white one and a black one – and they lived in a big, dark forest. The big, dark forest was very big and very dark. Of course, the white fairy was very good and the black fairy was not so good but she tried hard. The white fairy lived at the top of a very tall tree where the air was fresh and there were clear blue skies every day and the birds sang their songs and she was happy. She flew about all day helping others, wishing good spells and trying to do the best she could. And she did, everyone liked her.

But the black fairy lived down, deep down under the trees amongst the roots with the slugs, worms and other creepy-crawlies that lived in that part of the world. It was a dark place, so very dark and she just flipped and flapped about because she couldn't see very well. The black fairy didn't like her world because she felt so sad and she thought that there must be a better place than this. But she didn't know where or what this was. Feeling sad made her cross so she cast evil spells on all (those) around her. She wanted so much to be happy.

One day whilst she was casting her nasty spells (which she didn't like doing but heck, so what?) she flapped into a slug.

"Yuck," she said, "you are horrible and slimy."

"Yes, my dear," he said, "but I can't help my body; this is the way I am."

The fairy thought about what the slug had said and she felt sad and started to cry. The slug asked her what the matter was. He knew the black fairy didn't really mean to do bad things. The fairy said that she was very sorry for the hurt she had caused to all the living things down amongst the tree roots. This was her home, too, and all she had been was horrid and nasty to everyone.

The slug looked at the fairy and because he was kind and thoughtful he asked if he could help her in any way. The fairy thought about this and she suddenly had an idea.

"Kind slug, do you think you could help me find a way out of this dark and gloomy place?"

"Why, of course," he said. "Please follow me," and he slithered and slimed his way up and outward. Slowly, the fairy saw a light at the end of his tunnel.

"I can see a light up ahead; what is that?" she asked.

"Well, my dear," said the slug, "that is the top of my world."

So, the fairy, that did not really deserve the slug's kindness, flipped and flapped up and out of the slug's tunnel and into the bright blue sky. She thought how good it was, how the air was fresh and how she could hear the birds. Then she noticed that, sitting on the top branch of that very tall tree, was a beautiful white fairy and so she flew up to join her.

The white fairy and the black fairy became best friends and from that day on the black fairy decided she was going to be a good fairy. Everyone lived together happily in that big, dark forest which might not be so dark anymore.

The End.'

In case you didn't realise, I am the black fairy.

***

I never went back to see that therapist, so I never showed him my story. I found the sessions a little annoying because I wanted to talk about my marriage problems but the psychotherapist was fixated on my upbringing.

***

It's Manda's 50ᵗʰ and Jax is coming over and bringing her good American friend, Judy. It's going to be a riot. As soon as I collected them from Gatwick it was fun, fun, fun. Judy had never been to England before. In fact, I'm not sure she'd ever left the States so it was hysterical when she couldn't understand the driving on the wrong side of the road and told us the roads were actually paths compared to the massive four- or five-lane roads in Florida. We've managed to do everything that Jax likes – buy cakes from Forfar's mainly, and a visit to our Budgens supermarket – and all the time trying to hide from Manda so that we didn't spoil the surprise. It was just like school again when we used to play cops and robbers behind the hedges and jump out at each other with our pointy fingers: 'Bang, bang!'

***

I desperately want to keep everything normal for the sake of the children but, as the days go by, I'm finding it harder and harder and, anyway, I'm not sure what 'normal' is anymore. Growing up, as Jerome did, in a thoroughly patriarchal Irish Catholic family must have been hell. His father ruled the household and if the children complained, got upset or cried, there was a penalty.

***

Jerome is constantly out. When I ask him where he's been, he gets all shirty and says things like, 'For God's sake, why do you keep asking?' So, I stop asking and instead allow everything to simmer angrily inside me and go upstairs to write in my diary. This is a joy, actually getting all my thoughts from out of my head and onto a page. I recommend it. I look in my local directory magazine and there, in the middle pages, is a small advertisement offering counselling. She's a woman. I decide I'll give her a call, make an appointment; after all, I only need to go the once, just to make absolutely sure I'm not mad.

***

As I'm driving to my first session I realise she lives in the very same house that I learnt how to smoke a bong! Well, I didn't actually get the hang of that, but, anyway. I spend the first of these sessions in floods of tears with my next thought being that I can't afford to carry on. Of course, I do go back every week and slowly a whole new world opens up. After a couple of years of seeing Ruth, I know I'm not the dreadful person I thought I was.

***

Throughout all the times I've spoken with Ruth, I realise that so much is to do with my relationship with my parents. After my mother died in 1988, the relationship with my father never really improved in that we didn't become closer.

Like Jerome, my father was generous with material things but no good at all with emotion. I'm sure that being away from my parents at such a young age made me needy for comfort and love. Maybe I didn't have a lot of understanding about love and ended up choosing relationships that resembled my parents' marriage. On the plus side, I became a very strong, independent woman.

***

Ruth asked, 'Have you ever thought of seeing a solicitor? They don't charge for a first visit, you know.' It's got me thinking.

***

When I first smelt alcohol on Jane's breath during the day, possibly at school pick-up, a distant memory returned. It dawned on me that my grandmother's breath smelt the same when she came to my bedroom to kiss me goodnight.

It sort of crept up on my friend Jane, the business of going overboard with her drinking and smoking and everything else-ing. I don't know how she found the time with three young children and working as a teacher at a sixth-form college. It didn't help having a husband who was always up in London working or one that didn't really help with the children and I sometimes think that Phil stayed away on purpose because he didn't want the hassle of getting involved. It's probably a combination of all that that sent her over the edge. You try to help. You *want* to, but once someone is so entrenched it's impossible.

Jane is a raging alcoholic by this stage and has permanently green fingers, stained because she keeps losing her dope in the back garden and spends a lot of time crawling on all fours trying to locate the stuff. Whenever I try to go and see her so that her middle child and mine can play together, she invariably doesn't open the door. On the odd occasion I *am* admitted, she'll make me a cup of tea and I notice her mug is full of red wine. She turns up at school to pick up her kids with white powder round her nose and is arrogant enough to be smoking a joint whilst parked at the school gates. She spends days in bed and won't answer the door.

***

Jerome has taken the oldest to Barcelona and I'm here on my own with P who is being a trifle difficult.

Example: "I want to get out of the bath."

"Okay," I say.

"No, I don't want to get out of the bath."

"Okay…"

"Mum!"

"Yes, P?"

"Mum!"

"Yes, P?"

"Mum, I want to get out of the bath."

"Okay, do you want a towel?"

"No."

"Come on, P, I thought you were getting out of the bath."

"No!"

"Mum, I'm getting out of the bath now."

"Right, would you like a towel?"

"No, Mum."

And now I'm beginning to get a little annoyed. P gets out of the bath, demands a towel, troops downstairs and shouts at me:

"I want my own TV on."

***

Jane's husband, Phil, has told me that his wife has had sex with Jerome. I'm surprised it hasn't happened before, but maybe it did.

'How do you know?' I ask. We are on a train going up to London – him to work and me to see my father. P is with me and I'm stuffing her full of those red liquorice shoelaces. They take her an age to eat and she needs to concentrate, so I'm hoping she won't hear our conversation about her father and Phil's wife – not that she should remember anyway as she isn't quite five years old yet. Phil recounts he came home earlier than usual on Tuesday and saw them through the window. I feel sick because, apart from anything else, Jane's an alcoholic and is not in a good place and how awful that Jerome has taken advantage of her weakness.

Now that I know about her and my husband, all respect has gone and I don't know how to get that back. I feel sad that not only have I lost my friend but also H is likely to lose her friendship with their middle daughter, Els. I also feel deeply sorry for Jane and that Jerome has taken advantage of someone so vulnerable. Actually, no, I don't. I don't because, deep down, I know their affair has been going on for a very long time, long before her descent into oblivion and chaos.

***

It sends bad signals to the children when both parents don't agree, especially when it comes to discipline. Jerome doesn't support me in this way. His argument is that he's never at home so says he shouldn't get involved in discipline. When he *is* home, he hides away in his garage/study and we hardly see him at all.

***

Jerome and I are muddling through in our own stews. We are like two people in a boxing ring, dodging each other, darting one way and then another, avoiding each other. We're just not sure and it's as if we don't know each other at all.

I desperately want to leave this 'marriage', but I don't know how.

It took me a very long time to work out that grown-ups and people older than you are not always right. I just always assumed that anyone older than me must know a great deal more and that whatever they thought or said must be the right thing. It was because I was so useless at school, coming out with hardly a qualification to my name. If you're told you're stupid, then you believe it and I guess if your parents aren't around to give encouragement, that doesn't help either.

***

I loved to read stories to my H when she was little. Well, I loved to do that with both girls but with the age gap it's like having two only children. I start off with a classic book, AA Milne's *When We Were Very Young* and my favourite poem that reads like a prayer. It's called *Little Boy Kneels at the Foot of the Bed*; my mother read it to me when I was little. Because it was a prayer, I would kneel at the side of my bed as she read.

When I read it aloud to my girls, I change the words from 'I can see Nanny's dressing gown on the door' to 'I can see Nana's dressing gown on the door' because that's what they called Jerome's mother Jose.

With P I read all-sorts, but my favourite is *The Selfish Giant* by Oscar Wilde. P gets a little cross when I start to cry, which I do every single time I read the story. When I read to H she would go to sleep nicely after two or three stories. With P I could read endlessly, and she'd still be wide awake.

***

In adult life I have cried a lot but I don't know whether it's a good thing to cry in front of children. Everything I read and hear about says it is not. I think my oldest has suffered the most with my crying. Throughout her tiny, early life, I cried. Over these many years I have also screamed out hate and most of the hate and the crying was done at the same time.

***

There was one time when I just wanted to get away, probably because H and P were bickering. It was a Saturday afternoon and I decided to drive up to the Beacon where I might get some peace and quiet and lie in the tall grass surrounded by buzzing bees and gentle butterflies. All I got were those buzzing hand-held motorised aeroplanes. It was frantic up there.

I also take myself over to the cemetery where Jax's parents are buried. I like to just sit there quietly listening to nothing in particular – just with my silent nothing.

***

It's the day of H's confirmation and it really is glorious, sunny and warm. She got some great gifts including a beautiful Bible from my two sisters-in-law, the kind of Bible I would like to read. My father gave her a large silver spoon which I'm sure will be useful for something. We gave her a white gold crucifix with white sapphires and bloody Auntie Biddy gave a silly book called *Why I'm Being Confirmed*, which probably cost tuppence at the WI jumble sale. Although she'd been invited, she couldn't come, 'because I can't leave Lucy'. Lucy is a Norfolk terrier who she has brought up terribly, is thoroughly overweight and will immediately wee on your shoes whenever you arrive at her cottage.

***

H said that at school the teacher went round the class asking what everybody wants to be when they grow up. H said she wanted to be 'a wine consolidation unit person'. I'm not quite sure what this means but it made me laugh.

***

Jerome came home from work early the day before yesterday (Monday) because he wasn't feeling well. Went to work fine yesterday and today is laid up again and has been in bed all day. What is shocking is Jerome's lack of attention to the girls. P just went into his room and called, 'Daddy, Dad...' but nothing. H and I were concerned because his car was there but there were no lights on in the study or anywhere else in the house. I went back into the downstairs bedroom and there he was.

"Hey," I said, "why couldn't you just respond to P just now?"

"Couldn't speak."

"You're speaking okay now, though."

"Fuck off."

***

I am grateful that at long last I've found a house to move into for my girls and myself. Fingers crossed we'll be in by Christmas.

***

In my early diaries when H was two, I'd written how much we missed Daddy when he was away working. I wrote that in case one day H should read the diary so that she wouldn't see how her father really is. In that early first diary I was writing more for H than for my truth. I am frightened. Frightened about the future and how friends will be with me, but I *do* know I no longer feel able to maintain relationships with anyone who isn't there for me. I said to Ruth that for the first time I realise that I haven't really got many good friends. I have long-standing friends and I have acquaintances and because of my upbringing, I guess, I deal with everything by myself because I am not good at asking for help.

***

I live with my girls in a tiny two-up two-down right in the middle of a nondescript village so we can walk to all the shops and P can walk with her friends to school – she's now seven years old. The house is so small that I feel like a giant in it and keep imagining I'm actually living in a doll's house, but my house is called Freedom and I am in a new beginning.

The only problem I can see in this new and very different life is that I've got to be careful with money because, although I don't need to collect H from school until 6pm, I want to be home when P gets in from school at 3pm. So whatever work I do has to fit in around her school day. I help out at a local kindergarten, which brings in very little.

***

Once we've settled into the new house P tells me often she wants her big house again with the swimming pool and my oldest doesn't say a lot except for 'Yeah, Mum', in that teenage way she has sometimes.

Now that we're in our new life, I've taken out a small mortgage and have bought a brand-new car, a Citroën C3 Pluriel. She's called Muriel the Pluriel and I wanted something wacky to lighten our new life and have a bit of fun in. Muriel's roof comes right off and I thought that the girls and I would love to cruise in her, but the thing is, when you *do* take the roof off, you can't hear a bloody thing as the wind thrums the windows and you can't even hear the radio playing. Also, it only has two doors and it's meant to be clever because it's semiautomatic, but you still have to manually flick the gear stick in the direction of each gear change; for instance, bring the stick down for second and across for third, etc, so it's quite a ridiculous purchase.

***

In our new little house, there is a narrow hall with blue carpet and everywhere downstairs is brightly decorated. The sitting room is pink with a pink carpet and a strange stone hearth inset with a stone seat that no-one in their right minds would want to sit on. The only room's decoration I like is the dining room, which is a pale mint green and soothes me. This room has French doors leading out to my pocket-handkerchief garden, but I don't care about the garden. I don't do gardening. At the end of the garden is a wooden shed and a wall with a bank that leads down to a stream. An occasional trout glides past. I've always wanted to live in a house with a stream but that's only a dream. It is suburbia where we are because on the other side of the stream is the red and orange Royal Mail sorting office which is glaringly bright 24-7. Lovely view. No, it isn't. Just before I moved in, the council chopped down the three trees on the bank opposite, which would have been an adequate screen from the Post Office eyesore. I write to complain but you can't put back fully matured trees. They say the trees' roots were rotten. What rot.

To the rear of this house, I have a fledgling tree that I've called Christopher because a psychic once told me I had a son in spirit and, as I always wanted a boy called Christopher, I've decided this tree is him. I also have a little girl sitting on a swing high up in the oak tree on the other side of the stream beyond the wall of my new house. In any event, he was only with me for a few days – a fleeting shadow, and what of that little girl high up in the tree? I think that little girl is me. I find that comforting because she looks free.

Next door is a really dilapidated house that belongs to Jean and Joyce, twins in their 80s, except they don't live together. Joyce lives in London and will only come down occasionally. It looks like nothing has been done to it in years. When I creep past their rear window and sneak a peek, I can see that they still have the old gas lamps in the hall. I'm dying to have a look inside, but I don't know Jean that well yet and feel it would be too rude to ask.

There is an enormous fir tree in their garden and when the sun shines a huge angel appears on my garden shed. It has massive outstretched wings as if to say 'Come here for a hug'. It's comforting. It turns out that this tree was a tiny Christmas tree back in their day because this is the house they grew up in and which they planted out in the garden. When it gets windy in the autumn, I'm worried that this tall tree will fall onto my house, which makes me nervous. I work out that it would more than likely fall on H and P's sleeping areas and that's no good. My bedroom is at the front of the house, so I'd be okay. I need to pluck up the courage to ask if they would mind if the tree got chopped down. It is so large and tall that, apart from the shadow angel at the bottom of it, the rest of the garden doesn't get much sunlight. I'm more worried about it falling over, though.

After all that, I'm pleased to report that Jean was very good about this and the tree has gone. Their garden, too, is completely overgrown. Even the outdoor toilet is covered in ivy. Occasionally, Jean will come out and attempt to weed a patch and, although I don't say anything, I think to myself that really whatever she's doing is not doing a lot.

Our house is one in a long row of terraced houses, identical to the Victorian style, which were built for the workers building the railway line down to Brighton. We also have a row of terraced cottages on the opposite side of the road, but they are slightly bigger than my side and were built to house the managers. So, workers on my side and managers on the other or maybe the other way round? Having been privately educated, H cannot stand living here; she is a stroppy 16-year-old now and will not walk to the shops by herself in case she meets someone she knows, all of whom apparently 'live in enormous houses'. She spends a lot of time at her dad's, especially after the terrible rows we have. We *do* have a lot of arguments –arguments between H and I and arguments between H and P whom she calls a brat. It's so difficult with the nine-year age gap.

It's a whole new ballgame my two girls and I. Everything is my responsibility and it isn't easy. H and P are constantly bickering but I do have a routine with their father. They will visit him on a Wednesday evening and spend every weekend with him, that is Saturday and Sunday or, rather, Saturday evening through Sunday.

Chapter Twenty-Four

Without Me

My youngest daughter has just returned from a weekend with her father. I don't cope very well when she's away and she sometimes returns slightly dishevelled because her daddy doesn't really cherish her like I want him to. So, my little girl, whom I love beyond everything, will have small parts of herself crushed, demolished and shoved to one side. She will return all muddled and messed up and I will have to get her back, which takes days of nurturing, reeling her back in until we are together again. I'm too scared to say anything, as his response is usually, 'Yeah, yeah', and nothing ever changes. It's at times like these I feel alone. My friends don't call when I assume they telepathically know when I need them.

I get tired doing everything all by myself and there are certain places you can't walk in to by yourself – a pub, for instance –not that I would want to, but I think about these things. It is strange being on your own dealing with the everyday all by yourself. I also realise I'm not part of a gang, a coterie of friends; I'm more the outsider, on the edge. I look back on the days when I was young and carefree and what a gang I was in then. I am on the edges of things – the edges of friendships, the cusp of poshness.

***

My youngest loves to jump rope with a skipping rope, the type of jumping that requires a person at each end to swing the rope. I don't have a second person to hand so I tie one end to the doorknob, which seems to work okay. She also lines her teddies and dolls out on my front wall, which is right on this busy street. I don't know why she wants to play in front of everyone. The lovely guys at the butcher's over the road keep an eye on her.

***

I'm wondering if I should see Ruth again, my counsellor. Not sure if I'm dealing with things correctly with P. Not sure how much I can say to her before it becomes a rant from me. I do know that Jerome is not treating me respectfully and I'm not sure why this is upsetting me again because he never treated me properly in our marriage. I'm worried that this lack of respect he shows in front of the children will rub off on them and they'll start treating me and perhaps their friends the same. H particularly is a huge worry for me – she's always so angry and narky and I don't handle her well.

***

The latest row started when P wanted paper and I said, 'You know where it is so go and get it yourself'.

"No!" she screamed then started crying and shouting, 'You're stupid!' She threw the bin of pens all over the floor – I mean everywhere – threw things at me, threw her lemonade all over the sofa and then when I relented and got her own pad of similar paper from my cupboard, she tore that all apart. P is still hiccoughing now. I don't know how to handle this for the best. I turned off the TV and said she couldn't have it on again until she was in her pyjamas. She cried and screamed, so I said 'Okay, you can have the TV on but you get into your jimjammies at the same time. If you haven't done this within five minutes, the TV will go off'. She did it but in the meantime I'd run a bath, which she got into, then promptly got out of and went upstairs to put her school uniform on again! For Christ's sake, what do I do now?

"I'm not going to bed, you can't make me."

"Why can't I make you? Of course I can."

"You can't pick me up anymore."

And that's true.

I have just called P stupid, which is a word I was determined never ever to use. Calling her silly is fine but not stupid. I am not being nice, but P is not doing what I have asked her to do – 12 times now – which is to put her pyjamas on. That's all. She is in high heels, a skirt and a top and at six years old she needs her sleep on a school night.

Now she's crying or, rather, getting over the crying and hiccoughing and I am at my wit's end.

I have threatened: 'NO TV!' for P tomorrow morning and I must carry this out. I say I won't do anything for P tomorrow unless she says sorry to me big time. She hasn't and she's edged away from me in the bed we share when I read *Cinderella*.

P says she has two mums and two dads and has cried tonight because of the loss of her real mum and I said 'What about me?' and P said, 'You're my real mum, too, but my other mum is in heaven. Her car is a super-duper racing car'.

It is perfectly horrid round here and when I was in the old house I was SO looking forward to our new life of freedom.

My youngest daughter also has a couple of imaginary friends. The main one is called Jonathan and he is quite naughty and sometimes pushes her. The other is Goggles and they come from the Planet Yubber. Goggles seems to come and go a lot, but Jonathan is a constant. This morning, P cocked her forefinger to me and said this was 'bye bye'. I asked if this was from her dream. 'No', so she asked me to do the same to her, which I did. Strange, a bit like *E.T.* Jonathan eventually went to Paris and never came back.

***

I'm desperate to find inner peace but there's no inner anything in my new, single-parent life. Surely, I've done the right thing, surely? But in 2004 and throughout that year there were only brief windows of joy. My girls fought each other, mainly to get my attention, which they didn't want to share. I keep telling myself it will get better – it will – but all I want to shout is 'GET LOST both of you!' I'm scared that if I *do* say that they *will* get lost and go off to their dad's and won't want to see me anymore. I'm so frightened that they don't love me as there's lots of screaming, tears and hysteria. Now that he and I are separated, H can play one off against the other and, although I don't think she does this on purpose, I do think there is something in that. So, after the latest row when H tells me to 'Fuck off!' I say, 'Well, if you can't abide by my rules in my house then you'd better go and live with your father' and she packs a bag and leaves.

Chapter Twenty-Five

South Africa without me

I don't have any plans for a summer holiday this year but Jerome has made plans. He's going to take H, P and his friends, Joe and Kathy, to South Africa. Joe and Kathy were my friends, too, but that's okay. Some people say they won't take sides but quite obviously they do. Joe's brother, Paul, and his wife, Sue, live in Plettenberg Bay and we still have our apartment that we bought as a holiday home.

H is allowed to take her friend, Harriet. I feel crap and I'm not dealing with this well. P told me, 'Guess what, Mum? When I go to South Africa, Kathy is going to look after me when everyone else goes on a shark hunt'. Sharks? *Eeek.*

I feel sad that I can't afford a holiday like this and I couldn't go to SA on my own with my girls anyway. It's not that safe for an all-girls trip. As soon as I have this thought, I think people like Joe and Kathy are laughing at me. I think they snigger behind my back. Joe can't even look at me these days, but Kathy isn't nasty, she just isn't. The only holidays I can afford are the package ones like Tenerife (twice), Crete, Turkey and Sharm El Sheikh. They're okay with the kids' entertainment in the evenings, which gives me a break and a sex on the beach cocktail.

Chapter Twenty-Six

Signs

It was in February 2005 that I began to see signs, for instance, the huge crosses in the blue sky above. If I'm in my head I know that really, they are trails of smoke from the planes flying overhead, criss-crossing the sky, but in my heart I believe they are kisses from God, the universe (whatever you like to call it) to say that I am loved. So these kisses in the sky comfort me and are sent JUST for me! It is as if, after all these years, someone is saying: 'Come on, wake up, look around you and see the beauty that is everywhere'. I never really noticed before.

I am surprised at how few people look around; I mean, *really* look. I like to think there is magic everywhere. After all, there was that time when I was having a quiet rant in bed. The children were with their dad, which means it must have been a Saturday night and I was missing the children – but only a little bit – and was generally feeling 'poor me, there must be more to life than this'.

So, I started to talk to my mother. I do realise she's dead but I ask for her help because I was finding this being on my own business really hard and I really wanted more money, but what I very much wanted was for my mother to acknowledge that she hadn't really been available as a mother when I was growing up and I wanted her to say sorry.

I'm not making much sense, but I needed to know that she'd heard me, but how? I knew she loved birds and she also liked butterflies, except she stuck pins in the butterflies, which she kept in a glass case for display, so that's no good. The next day I was out in the strip of the garden hanging the washing on the line and from nowhere a little jenny wren flew and landed right next to me, I mean, RIGHT NEXT TO ME on the washing line. So, how does that work? Some magic is inexplicable.

***

I have always felt that there is something 'other' going on in my life but that otherness got squished out of me somehow during my marriage.

Do you think you can lose your instinct? I think you can and I did during my marriage because when someone tells you you're an idiot, mad and a drunk, you start to believe you really are and that there's no escape.

My instinct starts to come back when I begin reading psychic authors, the first of whom was the American author and psychic medium, John Edward. I also realise that I've always been interested in this other spiritual side and I want to get it back. I turned away from it when I had the children and a husband who was totally earthed and couldn't see anything other than what was in front of him, which in his case was a high wall.

I've got to try and turn my life around. So often I get trounced by the mundaneness of my every day and I've got to make time to *be* and to *think*.

***

I am now a fully qualified reflexologist, which is exciting. I can work for myself fitting work around my children. Everything I do must be like this because I will not allow my children to be latchkey kids. I want my children to remember their childhood and a mother who is always there and present with them. So, I will only do so much in order to maintain the equilibrium that H, P and I hopefully enjoy; I will not farm my children out to a childminder or to after-school clubs either.

Most of my reflexology clients are elderly and I go to their homes. It's sweet, actually, because I enjoy being company for them and having a little chat. Evelyn and Marjorie are sisters in their 80s who live together. They bicker and I worry about Marjorie who has a rather swollen tummy. Marjorie is gentle, I like her, but Evelyn is very difficult, constantly finding fault with Marjorie. Their feet – dearie me! I don't look too carefully and wash my hands a lot after their treatments.

The sisters' house is one of those 1970s bungalows with the avocado bath, basin and loo, patterned carpets in every room and, basically, a very simple, uncomfortable home. Single beds. I don't know why people choose to live so meanly. Why not have a double bed, go on – spread yourself out – spend some bloody money? But they are of that post-WWII rationing era where everything was austere and dark. Marjorie has never married. Evelyn has, but to look at them you'd think Marjorie was the marrying kind, being softer and, in my view, prettier. Evelyn comes over as a bitter, disappointed person and I guess they've both had a difficult life. Marjorie has moved in with Evelyn and I think Evelyn's bitter about that, too. Marjorie dies about a year-and-a-half after I start treating them and I honestly believe that my treatment helps her to keep going. We have lovely chats.

I am amazed by what some of my clients *don't* tell me during their consultation process. Vera suffers with dementia so getting her to the appointment at all is quite a feat in itself (no pun intended). During the course of our consultation, I asked if she had any urinary or kidney problems and she told me that she didn't. It turned out that she was having dialysis three times a week because of chronic kidney failure. Another client, Joan, neglected to tell me that she has Paget's disease and it was her daughter who told me three months after I began treating her. I can't understand why she isn't in pain.

I've got a new client, Joy, except she isn't a particularly joyful person; she's mostly full of fear. She's got conkers all over the corners of her house, which ward off spiders, apparently. She does nothing with her life but she is old now. She never reads, doesn't watch TV, she goes out occasionally with her daughter but usually doesn't want to. Joy told me today that sometimes she doesn't want to wake up. Goodness, I feel so sad that people live like this and don't help themselves even a little bit. Then there are her feet, flat with hugely swollen ankles like big leaden tree trunks.

***

Through reflexology, I meet an 86-year-old who has never read a book in her very long life. Never. To me, that is shocking. 'I just don't like reading', she tells me, but in her next breath, she says, 'I'm so bored. There's nothing on the telly'. She told me she only enjoys watching snooker on the telly (which is black and white) and darts. She has a bath twice a week on a Tuesday and a Saturday, has £1 meals from Iceland (how on earth are these meals made for one single pound and what is in it?), has no central heating in her house and during the winter months lives all day in her kitchen with her gas oven on and has exactly the same meal for breakfast and tea. But, hey! Who am I to say how she should live her life?

As I said, she's 86 and still alive, but is she *living*? Although she can be grateful for what I do for her, she more often than not would rather complain. One of my jobs is to get her cash – usually £250 every couple of weeks or so – but, boy, you should see her when I hand the money over. The whine of, 'Oh! You didn't get me any five-pound notes. How will I pay the milkman?'

Of course, she hadn't mentioned anything about getting five-pound notes or even a milkman.

***

My 50th birthday is coming up and, actually, I'm quite excited because for the first time in forever I've decided I will celebrate big time. I can't remember the last time I had a party. The one for my 40th seems eons ago now and I remember what Jerome gave me as a gift. It was a great big coat and looked very expensive but was made for a man because the buttons were on the wrong side for a woman. I teased him about it, but he didn't find it funny. I think this is how he thinks of me even now, with so little regard, or rather that he doesn't really think of me at all.

I've decided to go all-out so I've hired a marquee, which is to be set up in my titchy garden. It's coming with proper flooring, a dance area and even heating. Well, it is February after all, so it's drizzly, dark and cold – possibly not the best time of year for an all-out party. The celebration will be held on a Saturday night but, about a week or so before my big event, my oldest asks if she can have a party the night before mine on the Friday. 'Honestly, Mum, it won't be a big deal and, after all, you'll have the marquee already set up. I'm 17 and haven't had a party for ages'.

I am hesitant. Will they clear up properly before my party? P is very young to be in that kind of environment and my house is small with only one bathroom downstairs. This is my village; I have lived in this area now for, ooh, years – more years than I've lived anywhere else – India or London – and I know loads of people so feel that I'm in a safe place. Surely nothing could go wrong? I've pre-warned my neighbours and a couple of my male friends who live in my road – Wayne and Brett – who've said they'll look out for us and not to worry.

So, P and I hide out in the sitting room while H's friends troop round to the back entrance. It's fun; P and I are playing Old Maid but concentration is proving difficult because I keep hearing loud noises, cheers even, and I'm beginning to wonder why there is so much commotion outside and why the bathroom door is permanently being banged shut and locked. When I look out of the sitting room window, which faces onto the street, I am horrified to see huge crowds of young people queuing down the road and snaking around the corner into the high street. This is seriously bad as I know that there is no way all these people are going to fit into the marquee or even what's left of the garden and there'll definitely be queues back up the high street if any of them need the loo. Poor H is so upset because she doesn't even know half the people that have turned up.

Shit. I ring Wayne and Brett. I'm in full-on panic mode and thank God for Wayne and Brett because they arrive and, with gravitas, tell everyone to leave and, incredibly, they do. I can't remember if my oldest cries; she probably does because, for her, this is mortifying.

My counsellor, Ruth, tells me this is what she means about me giving my power away by allowing my oldest to hold a party the night before my own special occasion. The trouble is is that, at that time, I did that a lot, especially with the oldest. To me, it's the only way I can show I love her by giving her stuff and things because we're not very good at hugging, kissing and generally being affectionate. It's a shame really, and I am aware that this is all wrong.

***

I'm always in a rush, too. I'm very good – expert, actually – on rushing. I forget to enjoy the small moments. I'm always desperate to get to the next scene, the next episode of life and so I have got to learn to STOP. I'm going to really try. Since I left Jerome I feel sort of free and, somehow, I've got space to breathe. In Florida, Jax said to me, 'You need to stop, Penskew, you're always in such a rush'.

***

I'm trying – really trying – to find the good in the now ex-husband, but I can't, and in all the spiritual-type books I've read and continue to read, they talk about forgiveness, but I just can't forgive him and his shitty ways, his arrogance, the way he constantly belittles me in front of the girls – the lack of respect.

***

I had a very interesting time with my counsellor earlier. I spent most of the hour in floods of tears – again – and apologising – yet again – for using up her box of tissues. She says that's what they're there for and it's amazing that almost as soon as I sit myself down in her comfy armchair, the floodgates open and off I go. I've really started to depend on her and miss her when she goes on holiday. Recently I've been talking about my parents and whenever I speak about going to school at five years old or describe my mother, Ruth puts her head to one side and goes, 'Aww, it's so sad' or 'that must have been hard for you'. I'm a bit nonplussed by this because, as far as I'm concerned, it was normal. I know now that my upbringing *wasn't* normal but as a child you think everyone's upbringing is normal, don't you? At that age, you don't really think about anyone else let alone their upbringing and how it's supposed to be.

Ruth said, 'Okay, look in my basket, let's find what represents Jerome – choose as many as you like. I choose a scorpion, Batman, one of the dinosaurs, a robotic thing and a monster with six or eight arms all going in different directions.

"How about Sophie?" (an old friend from my flat in Highbury). A spaniel-type dog.

"H?" A plastic rabbit.

I was a mystical black cat and my father a big bear. All the items were in a semicircle looking inwards. I placed myself as the cat on the outside looking towards the items that weren't looking at me. Fascinating, because it was as if no-one was really that bothered about me, no-one cared about my feelings, my life.

It was a really good session.

Chapter Twenty-Seven

Wishes

There's a windowsill above my kitchen sink that houses Buddhas of all sorts, some in amethyst. There's an elephant too; several, actually, but my favourite item is a tiny, rubber fairy which comes from the oldest's Polly Pocket Cinderella palace. She's my fairy godmother and has a special place on that windowsill. It's to her that I look at when I'm making wishes. I can't go to my real godmother, Auntie Biddy (and at my age now, I am still expected to call her 'Auntie'), as she has disowned me.

I have lots of elephants – brass, wooden, marble, all-sorts – and it's important to make sure that their heads face away from a doorway to ensure no bad luck. With laughing Buddhas, you need to tickle their tummies to always have laughter in your life.

I wonder when my fairytale ending will happen, but maybe, a scary thought, I've already had it and I didn't appreciate it at the time or possibly I am in my fairy tale right now. I'm not sure if the fairy tale means I'm expecting a prince to come and sweep me off my feet, but I'm not sure I want to meet someone else at my age. Surely we are all a bit set in our ways now and I've been on my own for such a long time that I'm not sure I've got the room in my life for someone. I don't want to be at anyone's beck and call; I love my own company, being able to do pretty much what I like when I like.

I have now been on my own for over 16 years and longer if I go back to my married life. When I left Jerome, I made a decision that, as I obviously couldn't be a good wife, I was going to be a bloody good mother. I would be a very present mother and do the best I could in bringing up my daughters. It hasn't been easy, especially in the early days.

Chapter Twenty-Eight

My Bloody Aunt

She's a pain in the neck. Now that she's in her 80s she will only go to church if it's not raining or she will make the vicar come to her to give her communion on the pretence that she's too ill to get to church. She ends up in hospital regularly because that's the only place where she can find people to talk to.

I am rushing – again – to see my aunt in hospital because she's had yet another fall. How many is that now? Three so far this year and we're not even halfway through. In the hospital she is feeling sorry for herself, as usual.

"Oh, Penwen," she begins, "thank you so much for coming but could you nip back to the cottage and fetch some things for me?"

Oh, bloody hell, what? You mean I've driven all the way here, right past your flippin' cottage. Why didn't you ask me to do this on my way here? I don't say any of these things, though. I say nothing, keep my mouth shut (which is something I'm very good at) and make my way to her cottage.

When I get back, her voice is sly.

"By the way," she says, "a very good friend of mine in the village told me that the last time I was in hospital you spent over four hours in my cottage going through my things."

I thought she was joking at first because over the past year I have been toing and froing back and forth from hospital to cottage and cottage to hospital, but she's forgotten all that and is now referring to a supposed visit that took place over a year ago. She's never said anything before. Her cottage is literally a two-up two-down and, apart from being tiny, is chock-a-block full with ornaments and photos propped up on the mantelpiece. Even though there are photo frames around the sitting room, there are no pictures anywhere of the girls and myself. Instead she has photos of dead relatives like her mother, my father and, in pride of place, a photo of her now dead ex-husband. They were divorced before he died. Some of the pictures are in frames, others aren't, and they're scattered among the hotch-potch of china and ornaments.

There's just no way I could spend four hours, even two hours, in her house, but she no longer wants to see me and does not want me to continue being her lasting power of attorney. I am completely gobsmacked. Is this a little bit of dementia setting in? I'm furious that she should treat me like this when all I've ever done is try to help her. She could do with my help these days, too.

Incredibly, a few days later, I receive an official solicitor's letter in the post, but it's addressed to the house I lived in three years previously. Thank goodness the new owner rings the estate agent who finds me. The letter tells me that I am no longer Biddy's LPA and asks me to return her house keys and everything else that belongs to her and I do.

I write her a letter telling her what I think of her and how my father would be turning in his grave. What I would *really* like to happen is that when she gets to heaven they don't let her in. Ooh, and I hope my father has a few words to say but who am I kidding?

So that was a few years ago and then I had a phone call from her carers who I'd organised for her to have (when she was speaking to me, that is) to say they couldn't get hold of her and of course there was nothing I could do. My Aunt Joyce who lives in Devon phoned to say that Biddy would like to see me again after all, make amends and could I call her? I do. Nice chat, "Could you pop over to see me tomorrow?" she asks.

"Yes, of course," although I am a little nervous, but guess what? When I get there her 98-year-old male neighbour comes out to tell me that she's back in hospital again and he and I chat nicely and agree that my aunt is not easy.

I turn up at the hospital and all is fine.

"I'll ring you as soon as I get home, Penny."

Good – amends are being made – good, but a few days later when apparently she's been home for a couple of days and no phone call, Joyce calls to inform me and she is as shocked as I am that, after all, Biddy does not want to see me. Oh, brilliant! Dementia has definitely set in. I don't feel sorry for her though, although I suppose I should because what has been her life? It's been a life of nothing, of bitterness and lost opportunities and I have done so much for this disagreeable woman.

Chapter Twenty-Nine

White Wine

I love a glass or two of chilled white wine in the evenings and my particular favourite is a New Zealand Sauvignon. I cannot stand any wine that has Chardonnay in the title. It sticks in my throat and sometimes, as I'm opening the fridge door, I sing to the tune of the old R White's Lemonade TV advert where a man came tiptoeing downstairs and opens the fridge door to look for the lemonade, but instead of singing, 'I'm a secret lemonade drinker – R White's! R White's!' I sing, 'I'm a secret white wine drinker – I am! I am!'

I rarely suffer with a hangover, but in the past I have been known to lose my memory instead. In those days I was a good person to know if you needed to tell a secret to. I think it's so important to be balanced in life and to live in joy and I'm sorry that I am unable to be balanced in the quaffing of chilled white wine of an evening. I love it.

Chapter Thirty

The Wall

Jerome once told me that he'd built a wall around him so high that no-one could enter it and he could not get out – and that was that. End of conversation. Actually though, what of my own father? Did he nurture? No, he did not and how could he when he was not only physically absent but an emotional desert, as well?

I've just been going through some old family photos of my mother and her parents who I never knew and notice that her father looks very like my father. Is that what we've all done in my family and I've done it too? Married my father? *Yikes.*

Basically, I married my father who was as emotionally detached as my then husband and I guess because there wasn't much in the way of emotional love when I was young. I always felt that I was never allowed to show love – that it was wrong to show love in an affectionate way. It's that stiff upper lip thing again; 'one mustn't show one's feelings'. What I *do* know is that I love my children beyond anything and I loved my ayah Gwennie, so gentle and kind and softly spoken. Poor Gwennie had to put up with a lot from me when I was little, all that screaming watching my parents disappearing down the long driveway as they went off for club nights and pink gins. I never really knew my mother, not properly… and I love my dog.

***

There was a time a couple of years ago when I was on the home stretch after an hour's worth of walkies when I looked ahead and saw an old woman on a bench. She was just sitting quietly, way, way ahead. I wasn't frightened. I wanted to talk to her. She definitely wasn't my mother.

Maybe it could be Gwennie? As I got closer, she starts to disappear.

She disappears more and more until she's not there anymore. Every day I walk the same route hoping to see her again, but she's gone. Maybe that's someone telling me to stop looking for people who are no longer in my life – just STOP.

***

In my family, love, hugs and even kisses were definitely not the done thing. It was all tradition and how one ought to be, lots of unemotionalism. I think this goes back generations in my family. Not that I blame my parents, no, not at all; it is as it is, but I do wonder if that lack has made me unlovable. It is a constant at the back of my mind. As I said, I am not in a relationship and haven't been in one for a very long time and I wasn't in a relationship really, even when I was married. Is there something wrong with me? I keep asking myself: how did you manage to have two men in your life – father and husband – who are totally detached from their emotions? How did you do this?

I have difficulties with H and feel heavy-hearted and unsure. I feel morose, not depressed; just morose – I like that word. Things are not right, I have a fracture in my family and this is not how it is supposed to be. The thing is, I just don't have the oomph to put things right AGAIN. By this I mean I say sorry, but my sorry always has the added edge of: 'Sorry, darling, let me buy you this', or "Oh sorry, sweetie, I'll get that for you; no, no I'll pay for it'. Bloody years of trying to make everything okay in my strange, weird, not-right sort of way – and it is my fault. I tell H that I'm sorry for everything, that I don't know how to deal with stuff because I've never been taught and I'm sorry that I get it wrong sometimes.

My parents didn't parent. They followed the same cycle laid down by their own parents who didn't bother parenting either and on and on it goes. Jerome's father, the tyrant, followed his own way with a single mother and her own mother in a household of women in Northern Ireland and the catholic religious fervour. And me? I've broken the cycle…

On another occasion, Jerome confronts me about a disagreement between P and I. It floors me and I creep to the furthest edge of my sofa in the sitting room, far away, and every nasty thing that he's ever said comes hurtling back and smashes down on my head, my neck and my shoulders. My life – everything I thought I was over – oh, so over – all that, all the 12-and-a-half years later, the three years of fucking therapy – all that comes crashing back down on me and I'm a wreck – yet again – in the corner of my sofa in the corner of the sitting room, shaking, moaning and pathetically all by myself.

***

By 2011, I was holding down three jobs. As well as the reflexology, I still have my soup business, which I started in 2008 and which is ticking over very nicely. My soup business is called Sussex Soup and I deliver to my local Budgens supermarket and a few cafés round and about. I only make vegetable soups, but I have about ten different varieties. It's all very above board, even though my one and only bathroom is right next door to the kitchen. The council have been round and given me a five-star rating as well as a massive amount of documents, which they want me to read. God, it's so tedious, and I have to tick a lot of boxes on a daily sheet that needs to be maintained because at any time I could get an inspection.

I wrap a large scarf around my head to keep my hair out of the way; the worst thing is to find a lonesome hair in your soup. I don't know what happened when I lost an earring and had to start all over again. I still haven't found the earring. I wear gloves for chopping all the vegetables and my next-door neighbour has created a wonderful design, which I transfer onto labels. I've had to get those GSI numbers that give a barcode so that the supermarket can scan the pots and I also have to supply a use-by date so it really is very professional. It's annoying, though, when I get a call for an order on a Friday evening to be delivered the next day. In order to cool the soup down quickly, I fill the bath with cold water. Best of all is when it's cold outside, even better when it snows, and I can leave my industrial-sized saucepans outside covered in snow.

My third job is secretarial work for a local surveyor, John, who likes me to call him Roger. I've no idea why. I really enjoy this job; Roger is hugely amusing and has me in stitches most days.

Once a year, in November, I put on an Arts and Crafts fair in the village hall.

***

A long time ago I bought Jax a highly decorated dustpan and brush from a shop in the town where she lives in Florida. It was all crystals and beads and quite lovely. I knew Jax would appreciate this as it's a bit of a joke that she's fairly obsessed about cleaning and tidying up. If, for instance, you take a plate out in readiness for the toast you are about to make, you can be sure that plate will be returned to the cupboard before you can say 'Bob's your uncle'!

It was that which gave me the idea that I could decorate dustpans and brushes myself to sell, which I also do. I started to make all sorts of other things with beads – pull-string lights, beaded hairclips and bracelets.

Chapter Thirty-One

My father dying

My father has been terribly ill for over a year already. I don't know why he gets so breathless all the time. Does this go back to his smoking days? He's 80 now and he stopped smoking at 56 once Mummy's second bout of cancer was diagnosed.

Last year we discussed the possibility of moving in together, that I would sell my house, he'd sell his London flat and we'd buy somewhere local to me that had an annexe for him. An excellent idea and I liked that he'd be right next door to us should anything happen. Of course, there's nothing available in my area and I'm concerned that I just cannot visualise my children, my father and I together in a future. I can't see us all in the same building.

I began to compose a letter to him to encourage him to get his spirit back because basically he's given up. I say, 'Spirit is what will pull you through, please try', but I don't send the letter because in it I've also told him that I love him and I thank him for being my father but I'm not sure he'll understand never having told me he loves me himself. Not once. I am sad, too, that there is no mention of me on my mother's gravestone, nothing saying 'Beloved mother to…' or just 'Beloved mother'. Nothing, nada, niet. It just says 'Beloved wife of… and my father's name. It also says 'Safely home', which I think is lovely but when I ask my father about it he just says that he saw it in a book and it had no real meaning.

My father just gave up on living. If only he'd just tried a little harder to not eat so much Ferrero Rochers, Jelly Babies and winegums, which he pretty much lived on despite his type 2 diabetes.

He wondered why he kept falling over and I think it's that older generation thing. He would never drink water, preferring a gin and tonic instead. There were plenty of signs a good while before he actually went. There was that time at London Victoria station, for instance. I'd come up on the train for my usual visit. We would meet at the station and then go up the two escalators to where Garfunkel's restaurant was situated. For some reason one day, Daddy refused to come down the escalator.

"What do you mean?" I asked him. "We've done this loads of times before."

"I know, I know," he says, "but the height frightens me and I can't do it. Let's find the lift."

Well, there wasn't a lift or one I could find, but the next thing was that he decided to smash his way out through the fire doors.

"No, Daddy! You can't do that!"

"Who's going to stop me?"

Shit. He did it and I meekly followed, completely panic-stricken. Suddenly we were on the metal fire escape and down below were security men shouting up at us, but extraordinarily, he got away with it.

It was shortly after that episode that he got stuck in the bath. He just couldn't get out and he was there for 12 hours. He tried everything: putting a towel under himself to get a grip, filling the bath with more water on the assumption he would float up –but nothing. In the end, once he started shouting and managed to get the attention of other flat dwellers and his next-door neighbour who had a key, a rescue was made. Why do a lot of old people have mobile phones that they keep switched off and out of reach?

Almost at the end of his life, although I didn't know it then, he kept the London Ambulance Service on high alert. They could almost have been his private chauffeur service if the hospital was where he lived. On one day alone he called them out three times. It was no surprise at the third time of calling that they refused to come out, or rather, they *did* come out, but insisted he had to remain in hospital and not make his escape. They told him that if he decided to leave, the service would not help again.

This whole sorry saga started because my father decided he no longer wanted to be in St Thomas' Hospital. St Thomas' is like a whole town within a building. It is labyrinthine. There are masses of corridors with passageways going off like a vast arena. There's an M&S, so I go here first to buy the Jelly Babies my father seems to live on and a sandwich because, I have to say, the food in the hospital is completely disgusting – even worse than school food.

When I get up to my father's ward he makes an announcement.

"Penny, you have to get me out of here."

"What? You can't be serious?"

"It's no good," he says. "You need to get a wheelchair. I need to get back to the flat."

Oh, for fuck's sake. "Daddy, I really don't think–"

"Yes, we can."

I am embarrassed but dutifully go off to get a wheelchair. I am so pathetic in my obedience to my father. When I come back, I say to Daddy, "Don't you have to sign some papers in order to be able to leave here?"

"Haven't got time to wait around for that."

Bloody hell. God knows how I managed it, and God knows how I got my father into the wheelchair although he can still walk, just about. Off we go down to the ground floor where we manage to flag a black cab and then it's a short trip to his Victoria flat. Once inside, which took forever, I notice something brown oozing out of the bottom of his pyjamas. So now I know he's incontinent and I am cleaning him up. *Jeez, I never thought I'd have to wipe my father's bottom.* My poor father; all his dignity gone. His pride gone. He is a shadow of his former six feet four self.

I arrange for a carer to come in three times a day, to get him up in the morning, get him something for lunch and then make sure he's in bed in the evening. Of course, my father who has been used to waking and getting up at 5.30 every morning is not used to having to wait until the carer arrives at 8am and then the carer will turn up at 5pm to put him to bed. So, he's a crosspatch and complains endlessly… but this is where those ambulance calls come in because he isn't coping, he is seriously ill.

Being back in his flat doesn't last long and I am terribly cross/angry/hurt with him. He's not being very kind, he's being selfish and I don't know why I never realised this before. He's having a go at me a lot.

"Why have you put me in hospital? You promised you wouldn't."

I explained that it wasn't me putting him in hospital.

"You keep falling over all the time, your blood pressure is terribly low and the ambulance had no choice," I tell him.

He cries that he wants to go home.

I say, "And how am I supposed to do that?" and his response: "In a taxi, of course."

"But you can't bloody walk!" I make it very clear that he isn't helping himself. I don't stay long as I'm fuming. He doesn't understand or is not wishing to understand. Obviously for him (and me) the nicest ending would be in his flat but his flat is not my memory of a family home. My father has never been a family man and I am sad to say this but by this stage it had been a year-and-a-half since he saw his granddaughters.

In the meantime, I've found a lovely place for him to move to in Worthing. He'll be near bloody Auntie Biddy, too, and me but Biddy whines all the time.

"Oh, I beg of you, don't send him down here. They won't accept him, you know. He'll be sent straight to Worthing Hospital, which is a dreadful place." She's not making sense either.

He's back in hospital again and the staff have said that he'll be transferred to the Royal Brompton Hospital for more tests because basically he's not fit enough for the heart operation they want to perform. He's anaemic for starters. He's not helping himself, he doesn't eat and all he does is get cross and complain, mainly to me. I have been up twice in the week to see him, but conversation is difficult. I don't feel comfortable and I don't think Daddy believes he's as ill as he actually is. I don't have good thoughts about my father but then my next thought could be totally different. What I will find difficult is going up to London regularly to sort my father out. I feel I am putting my life on hold to cope with him. I don't think that's fair but I don't think I'm being fair either, sorry.

I have decided that I can't keep going up and down to London and carry on with all the jobs I have. I stop the soup-making and reflexology but I carry on with the secretarial work because I can fit that in during the evenings and John (aka Roger) is very understanding.

I am mourning my father already. I have cried loads and am thinking back to all the good times. He was a good man but a man of his time and I'm already talking about him in the past tense. I'm going up again tomorrow, Friday, and I don't have good thoughts that he'll ever make it back to his flat again but I do not want him to suffer as he has done anymore. This situation has been going on for a long time, since May and it's November now. All I want is for my Daddy to go graciously and with dignity. None of this is happening. There is no dignity at St Thomas', which is probably the same as in any hospital, but I have said to his current nurse that my father is a very private man and I ask if he could be moved to somewhere perhaps more private. Later that day, she rings me to say they've managed to find a quieter ward. How nice is that, to go to all that trouble? I want my Daddy to be comfortable and to have a really peaceful end. Auntie Biddy flitters and flutters around; she really is a pain but I think I have learnt a bit of patience.

I'm nervous about showing my feelings to my father but desperately feel I need to say something – anything – to make sure my father understands that I love him, just in case he doesn't come through the operation he's about to have. Nurses are coming in and out, my father isn't really there and so I brave it and say, 'I love you, Daddy'. Oh, that was good, so glad I said that. Phew. His answer comes rather shakily, 'Me, you, too'.

It's December now and I just can't summon any energy. I'm flat and feel just terribly sad about my father. Such a huge individual is now reduced to horribleness. He's a shell of his former self and I wasn't very good today in the overnight emergency recovery suite that he is resting in after his heart op. I am shocked at the sight of him looking so frail and seeing his open chest wound (or was that my imagination?) I couldn't bloody well stop crying – not so openly, though. Daddy stroked my face, he's never done that before, and it was such a gentle gesture, so beautiful. I kissed his hand; he's agitated but can't speak for all the tubes, looks awful and, frankly, he's never ever been in such a direct critical situation before (not in my memory, anyway). I don't want to think that when I leave the hospital today this picture of him will be my last memory because he just doesn't look like my Daddy anymore.

***

I am a dutiful daughter, I am doing right by my father and I also remember my Louise L Hay book about health and how problems with the heart can mean a hardening of feelings, lack of love, self-love, etc., I do sadly feel that this reflects my father, but he is also a man of his time.

I am a dutiful daughter and I start to pray and ask that my father's end comes soon, like now, and I say, 'Please, in goodness and love and Ferrero Rochers, Jelly Babies and winegums, please make my father's end come quickly. Amen'.

It doesn't. On and on it goes: the constant visits to my father in St Thomas', getting clean underwear, collecting his cheque book and turning the heating down. His internal stamina is unbelievably strong but he doesn't help himself and he's still bloody alive… but only just. He wants me to leave today because 'you're annoying me', so I don't want to visit anymore. What's the point? I shout out at the universe, *'Please, take my father into your loving arms and take great care him!'* It's all too late, he's having a terrible death where I'm sure it's possible to have a good one, but he really gave up.

Frankly, my father wanted to die; he didn't want to continue living a life that was not a life. Having had this huge life in India where he was highly regarded, this 'old' life – 'old' as in age that he now had – was definitely not for him.

Eventually, my father was able to move to a care home in Worthing where he could be properly looked after 24-7. There was no way he'd be able to return to his flat and my father and I come to the conclusion that the flat needed to be sold in order to meet the staggeringly high fees. He thought he was going back to his flat but that not possible, so a transfer by ambulance was organised.

***

It's Wednesday and I drive over to Worthing to see him. I try to go three or four times a week. The home is a really nice place, very modern and Daddy's room has a large window, which overlooks the garden with a few trees and plants. It's nice, but I do wish the nursing staff would stop calling him Dearie and Darling. It doesn't suit him and I can see him wince, poor Daddy. The nurses have just shown me his stash of sleeping pills – 10 bloody boxes of them with five sheets of pills in each one, which they have confiscated. They treat him like a naughty schoolboy.

"Honestly, Daddy," I ask him, "where on earth did you get them from and why have you got so many?"

"I've been getting them for years from a friend in Calcutta," he says, all casual. On another day we have a marvellous conversation about the monkey he sees in the tree outside his window.

I said, "Does that remind you of Jimmy in Assam?"

"Oh no," he says in all seriousness, "this monkey is green so completely different."

The best story of all, though, was on one of my visits when I walked into his room:

"Hello, hello," he said to me. "Yes, I'm back from London now. Spent the night in the flat but I'm back here now; what's this place called? It's not a hospital."

"No, it's a nursing home."

"Oh yes, very nice and I'm back in the same room here as I was in before, extraordinary, but you know I went all the way up to London in a white Rolls-Royce?"

I'm trying not to giggle because of course he hasn't been anywhere.

Then he continued, "You know, when we were building towers – huge towers…"

I don't have a clue what he's talking about but, in a way, although this probably doesn't sound right, if my Daddy *has* to die, which of course we all do, I'm glad he is dying this way, being in his own happy world. The last time I saw him he told me that he had to go to work and to 'please go', over and over again and, after touching his hand, I left as he turned to face the wall.

***

All those whole bags of sweets you munched on – Jelly Babies, winegums, plus the packs of 20 fags – taking yourself off to bed in the afternoon having never got over the habit of an afternoon's siesta from your India days. I guess the sweets eventually took the place of cigarettes when you gave them up. I suppose that's better than the endless smoking. It's funny, but when I was young I never smelt the smoke or was bothered by it. In fact, I was determined to smoke just like you and I did.

***

I guess it took about two years for him to die all told and during that time I'd like to say that we got to know each other, you know, really bonded, but of course we did not. On his almost deathbed it was stiff upper bloody lip – STILL?

Once he died, I didn't cry for my father; I did not cry at all. Even now, I don't feel his presence around me either. When my mother died I was terrified that she would haunt me and say 'I told you so' when my marriage broke up. 'You made your bed, now lie in it' or similar. The night before her funeral I made Daddy keep his bedroom door open and the hall light on. I really thought she might appear in my bedroom but it wouldn't be as a gentle soul. It would be as a ghoul, a horrid apparition and it was terrifying. When he died, a lot of my huge regard for him died with him. I started to see him as weak, as a person who would do anything not to rock the boat.

There wasn't much to clear up. He had left everything neatly filed and he only kept what he needed. No bulging messy files and papers like my mother. Nothing was out of place, that's what he was like in life too. No excess.

When I asked my Auntie Biddy what she would like as a memory from my father's flat, extraordinarily she chose a small, cheap, shallow, china dish in which lay cheap, dusty, plastic flowers. Maybe that's how she sees herself?

***

I'm feeling sorry for myself, I know, but I've been feeling sad all day today because it's Daddy's birthday and he's been gone for over a year now, although I sort of lost him ages ago. Been to see his plot at Worthing Crematorium and have asked for his help in finding me a house. I don't know, there was a cigarette butt on top of his urn

174

plot, which made me chuckle because of course he used to smoke heavily and I like the idea that it might have been his – smoking on his birthday!

Part Three
Growing

Chapter Thirty-Two

Return to India

Before my father died, we had spoken of my dreams to revisit all the places of my growing up. So, in the year after he passed, I returned to India with H and P. I had told them a lot about India over the years and they were very excited.

I had a small pot of my father's ashes, some of which I wanted to sprinkle at my mother's graveside – Bhowanipore Cemetery in Alipore – I have not visited since her funeral – and the remainder at Phulbari, the tea estate he loved so dearly. Of course, with my father not showing emotion, I can only say I think it was his favourite place. He and I never discussed it.

So, big plans are afoot. I write to the chairman of the company where my father worked for 40 long years (and I think about the lousy pension he received after having grafted all that time and being No2 in the company, the only white person left). The reply comes back that they would be delighted to host my girls and I and that we will stay at Tollygunge Club and travel to Assam to stay on the very tea estate of Phulbari. It's going to be immense. So all is set, flights, seats and it's business class all the way. You see, I've come into a bit of money having sold my father's London flat and I'm damn well going to do this properly and in great comfort. I had to keep stopping to remind myself to take everything in, no rushing and, you know how good I am at rushing, because I wasn't sure if I would ever return again.

The first thing I noticed in Calcutta was that everyone is Indian. I know that sounds silly but it was a shock because in my young day, Tollygunge Club, for instance, was mostly white. It was ironic that here we were staying at Tolly and we were definitely in the minority, the only white three. At the same time, I'm pleased that India has returned to her independent roots.

Everywhere is so much busier than I remember. Tolly Club was almost unrecognisable; it's more a hotel than a club now but the swimming pool is still there and we have to wear those ridiculous rubber caps that take me straight back to my childhood when I was the only child forced to wear them. 'It's to protect your ears, darling', as my mother would say.

We've been given a driver, Dinesh, who speaks really good English and I splutter my few remembered bits of Hindi, pigeon Hindi. We're off to the cemetery to see how Mummy is and I do hope my parents are proud of me in doing this for them. I really want to do the ashes thing by ourselves, you know, just quietly bury some ash, but it's not possible. We are surrounded by malis (gardeners) and someone called Jackie has arrived from the company to escort us, so that idea has gone out the window. Mummy's grave looks splendid – I reckon it's been spruced up in readiness for our arrival and I give the malis some *baksheesh* – quite a lot, actually.

Not much is familiar in lovely Calcutta or Kolkata as it is now called. What *is* the same is the Flurys pastry and chocolate shop that has been around forever, also the New Market, which is not new at all and has been rebuilt after the fire; was that in 1988? My girls and I are just having the best time, making new memories, and I'm so glad I persuaded us to buy special notebooks to keep a diary. Every night we write up our day and I give thanks. I've started to do that – being grateful for my every day and writing down my gratitudes.

The next morning we fly to Assam, which is only a 55-minute plane journey and then we find out it's another 4.5 hours of driving to get to Phulbari. *Oh gaad!* The roads are a mess, untarmacked, pitted and potholed. I am amazed at the volume of traffic, not only of buses, tuk-tuks and cars but cows with their thin bony hips sticking out, dogs wandering or snoozing in the dust on the side of the road, goats and buffalo also stick thin, pigs, ducks, geese, egrets and tiny shack houses far worse than I remember them. Our driver is crazy, driving too fast, and we bounce dangerously into all the potholes.

At long last we arrive and Phulbari is hardly changed. It has the same gravelled driveway with the wide, white entrance gates but the verandas are now enclosed and the entrance itself has wrought-iron shutters. There's a front door. The manager of the tea estate, SK and his wife Jayshree, greet us and are kindness itself. We visit the factory but nothing there is familiar. The chungs for drying the tea are now enclosed and I had no recollection of the factory itself, which SK said has all been modernised. The tea is fair trade and everything else trade certified.

We're to have a tour around the tea garden today and H and P will get a chance to pluck tea (two leaves and a bud, remember?) Today when the pluckers have a break they'll be refreshed with hot tea and salt to rehydrate them. We visit Thakabari Club, which is looking rather sad and forlorn and much smaller than I remember, but no swimming pool?

"No swimming pool, SK?"

"No, there never was one here."

That makes me worry for my memory, but as we walked down towards my disremembered pool there was a clear outline of where the pool would have been. I see a noticeboard on the wall with my father's lifetime membership. On our tour of the Estate, there's the Rome bridge and there are dedications to all the managers who ever worked here.

At every tea factory we visit, we are presented with pure silk Assamese shawls. I'm pretty sure I can make a whole set of curtains with them. Finally, we get the chance for a boat trip down the same old Borelli River that my parents and I, together with all the other families whose parents worked on the tea gardens, spent so many joyous occasions on.

I've still got the pot with the remains of my father's ashes that I want to sprinkle here in the garden. I've decided by the swimming pool, but this is proving tricky. As the daughter and granddaughters of a much-loved and respected tea planter, everyone wishes to fete us, show us around and not for one minute are we left alone until we retire to bed, which is late and it's pitch dark outside. I don't have much time to think, to reminisce and to have a good look round and I'm sad about that now.

In the late afternoon on day two, P and I manage to have a swim in my father's old pool where the signs and the pool itself are unchanged. I manage to sprinkle the rest of Daddy's ashes over by the hedge so he'll have a nice view of the surrounding landscape and the rice paddies below. The other reason I'm sprinkling his ashes here is that I don't want to be seen. I don't want a huge fuss and crowds of people standing around ogling me, which was the case when I added his ashes to my mother's grave. The swimming pool is hidden behind a hedge, so I hide.

From here we briefly go back to Kolkata and then on to Delhi, the Taj Mahal and Fatehpur Sikri. The girls and I have gone quiet as we realise it is almost the end of our time and we've left the places that were home to me. I visited the Taj Mahal and Fatehpur Sikri a lot when I was young, mostly with friends who had come out to visit. I treated these visits a bit like 'Oh, let's go to the beach today, shall we?' A little bit cocky or like a visit to Disneyland.

On our last day we each decide to get a henna tattoo done on our feet. I wanted something delicate like a butterfly and instead have ended up with a huge, intricately designed floral mass of swirls and dots and every time I look down I think I've got poo on my feet.

***

My life starts to come together in 2012. Just little things at first like our trip to India. I begin to put into practise everything I've learnt spiritually, you know, all the books I've read, the mindfulness courses, etc. I start to meditate every day, first thing in the bed in the morning and before fully awake, stretching myself out long and wriggling my toes.

Once up I then do a 10-minute yoga routine, which becomes routine in itself. I am up and ready to go by 7.00 in the summer months and as soon as it gets light in the wintertime. Obviously now that I have my dog my daily routine is even stricter because I know I'd have a whiney dog if I'm not raring to go. Yoga becomes difficult to do because as soon as I go into Downward Dog, Tolly decides that that's a good time to lie down across my mat, but then I can't go into plank because I'll crush her. I'm always in bed by 10pm. With all this new spiritual practice, I do have a problem with the looking in the mirror business and giving myself compliments. I try.

I don't feel my father around me – ever or at all. On the other hand my mother, with whom I had a strange and uneasy relationship, surrounds me and gives me guidance. I saw a psychic a couple of years ago who said that my mother was very busy wherever she was looking after lots of children. Perhaps that's penance for not looking after me.

***

My favourite season is winter. I love the cold, the dark early mornings, the early dark nights, lighting a fire and drinking my glass of Sauvignon or the occasional brandy and soda, but best of all I love a thunderstorm. I love thunder and lightning and the rage of the skies, it clears the air and it clears my head. When I was little and always scared when it thundered, Mummy would say that it was Peter and Paul playing marbles in heaven.

Chapter Thirty-Three

Significant Other

I don't have a significant other in my life and that's okay. Sometimes I worry that I'm becoming a hermit because I'm not that bothered about going out and after all this time I still enjoy *EastEnders*, another habit. These are the two programmes I started watching when I breastfed H – *Neighbours* and *EastEnders* – which would infuriate Jerome as they conveniently came on when he would arrive home from work and when H needed a feed. I love *The Real Housewives of Beverly Hills*, mainly for the shock factor of their immovable faces.

I love my superking-size bed and wonder if I should change the mattress but, anyway, I only take up a tiny portion of the bed. Tolly stretches over the rest. I am very aware that life is passing by in a rush now that I'm older and I need to pay attention, which is very easy to do on my Tolly walks although it's a struggle these days to walk sensibly through the mud and wet.

Chapter Thirty-Four

My Club

I'm a member of a local spa club, which I try to get to three times a week; at least that's what I tell my friends when they ask but usually I can only manage it twice. I swim for 45 minutes and I've bought myself a waterproof MP3 player – a very basic variety – and waterproof headphones so I can listen to Paolo Nutini, Van Morrison and Kirsty MacColl while I swim breaststroke. I can't do the crawl if I'm listening to music as the headphones keep falling out of my ears. They're on a very long lead and get caught up and wrapped around my legs. I am a strong swimmer and was champion in my school two years in a row, not that that says much when there's only 10 in a class. It was kind of what I expected everyone would assume, that I'd be a good swimmer, what with my Indian background and having a pool, although I have no idea why I would come to that conclusion. I want to say because of my Indian upbringing but I wasn't really brought up, at least not by my parents.

Even though school was years and years ago, I still have that competitive edge and a need to win. If I think someone is swimming faster than me at the club, I will speed up to beat them. It's ridiculous because they haven't got a clue what I'm up to and couldn't care less. The other day I was happily swimming up and down and out of the corner of my eye I spotted an older chap who'd turned up completely naked, he'd forgotten to put on his swimming trunks! I notice that people, women mainly, just sit chatting at one end of the pool. There's not much rigorous exercise going on in the swimming/spa area. They come in for a very expensive spa day wrapped up in their white cotton robes and white slippers where they spend five minutes in the sauna, five in the steam room, then lie on the loungers and look at their phones, have a leisurely swim and then go off to the restaurant for a huge lunch. The men mostly have pot bellies.

Chapter Thirty-Five

Santorini

P and I are on holiday and sometimes I like to make up stories of the people I come across. This time we're in one of the beautiful Greek islands, Santorini – literally a jewel – a shiny and bright blue sapphire in a blue sea. It's also volcanic with black sand, which might seem nice to you, but it made me feel dirty as soon as I stepped onto it. So I didn't.

I much prefer lounging by the pool with the hanging pink, white and orange bougainvillea flowers that are dripping over the white arches where beneath are people enjoying a leisurely breakfast. Of course the first thing I don't understand is, *Why, oh why, do the English abroad pile their plates high with a typically English fry-up?* Being that we are on a Greek island the 'fry-up' is not exactly the best because this is not what Greeks cook. It is beyond my comprehension that the English continually want to fatten themselves up (and, sadly, a lot here are very fat). There is fruit, yoghurt and a hundred different options to choose from but, oh no, 'We're on 'oliday, luv, so a fry-up it is!' Don't get me started on the boozing... well, actually, you can but I'll come to that later.

I make up stories about the families I see. My life has changed yet again and I'm no longer the person who endlessly stands in the pool with her legs apart to allow the youngest to swim through them, slowly edging my legs closer together to make it harder. Then there's bat and ball, throwing and catching and dropping coins to the bottom of the pool for P to pick up. My suntan is not the all over kind that I dream about and that everyone else seems to come home with, I'm more the hotch-potch variety.

Blimey, an Adonis has just arrived; this Adonis of a man is quite simply gorgeous, with his eight-year-old daughter. *I'm over here, helloooooooo..?* Where is Mrs Adonis, then? Ah-ha, damn! There she is, completely stunning; slim, trim, tiny bloody waist, shiny hair and looking beautiful – perfection. So why aren't they doing things with their child together? I suspect that it's because she's just too damn beautiful. I do notice, though, that none of the families do anything together as a family. How strange.

I play the role of the watcher, watching the goings-on with the so-called happily marrieds or the possibly nots. I look around and realise that even though I am a single parent here I am more of a family than they will ever be. There was also that time when I was being taken around a potential house by an estate agent. I showed an interest but she came back to me later that day to say, 'The landlady does not consider you to be a proper family'. Truly shocking.

When I go on holiday these days on my own I take my children with me in the form of rings, which have their birthstones. I also take my mother and wear the last gift she ever gave me, which was a pair of earrings: paste diamonds. I always need to wear odd numbers regardless of anything, so on my fingers I will have either three rings or five, seven or nine and it's the same with bangles and bracelets. I've no idea where this obsessiveness about odd numbers comes from but I guess it has something to do with bringing luck into my life or possibly comfort.

Nancy, who's an anthropologist and a professor, says wearing an amethyst stone in any form is a protector against alcoholism so I wear amethyst a lot.

Chapter Thirty-Six

Holidaying Alone

I feel overwhelmed, but I do breathe in and out. It's because I don't speak to anyone and no-one speaks to me.

I'm staying at the posh Pod Różą Hotel in Kraków. This is my first holiday alone. The hotel, although very upmarket, is quiet, dark and silent. Is there anyone actually staying here? When I go to the bar there's no-one else there and last evening at dinner I was pretty much the only person eating; I felt like I stuck out like a sore thumb. I was embarrassed and it was not relaxing.

Tonight, I'll nip over the road and buy a bottle of white wine to keep in my room – there's no point sitting at an empty bar, after all. Kraków is fabulous – lots of ornate churches heavily decorated with gold and a stunning market square just around the corner from my hotel.

This is the first time I am without the children and it feels quite odd. It's only a few days but I don't feel relaxed. I find it hard eating a meal with no-one to talk to, but I'm going to have to get used to this because this is my future. The girls will be off doing their own thing before I know it and quite right, too. *So, Penskew, think about it and put that in your pipe and smoke it*, except I don't smoke anymore.

***

I've become a lot more thoughtful, patient. I am a watcher of myself but not in a critical way. I am a pretty healthy person all told. I have friends who have had hips and knees replaced and it staggers me that I have a particular friend who has had both knees replaced at the same time and doesn't equate the fact that she'd worn her knees out with being thoroughly overweight. I have never ever broken any part of my body in my life, but I have got high cholesterol, which pisses me off and occasionally I have high blood pressure, too.

I do get immediate payback when I start thinking in egotistical terms. Take the other day, for instance. I was out to lunch with friends who'd all been suffering with flu, colds and coughs and there I was thinking: *Gosh, I haven't been ill for years and years* and then, blow me, two days later I come down with some cold/flu lurgy and am literally laid up, all shivery and cold. So, you see, you have to be careful how you think. I get scared because nothing really awful like a serious illness like cancer, for instance, has happened to me or, God forbid, to either of my children. I get scared at that thought and I really don't want to die yet. I want to be here for grandchildren, fun, more travel, experiences and curiosity.

I reckon it is so important for good health to be curious. I love to learn new things, which is why I read a lot and why I love to go on courses. I have read endless books on positive thinking: karma, dharma, prana and yoga. I definitely think there's something about all of them. There is. It isn't true that just because you have a positive mindset everything in life will be all hearts and flowers. I've studied stuff, too – NLP EFT, reiki I and II, reflexology, mindfulness on its own and mindfulness in yoga – on and on it goes… I've also had a ton of counselling, so really I should be a perfect human specimen. Ha! Of course, I am anything but…

Chapter Thirty-Seven

Karma

I do believe in karma except there are a few people I know who have not had their karma yet. What I *do* know is that when I have a nasty thought about someone I always worry that something bad is going to happen to me so I quickly say 'Sorry' out loud to no-one in particular.

I love the otherness, for instance, of my walks in the woods and I think I see shapes and tree trunks that look like whales and hollowed out trees that are perhaps home to goblins. I see the wise woman bush in my garden who I greet every day. I've decorated her with fairy lights and pat her on her head to say thank you for being so wise. I don't know why. When I'm at my club for a swim and sauna, I have Peter Pan just up there in a tree.

Across the three fields in my second house after divorce, the railway line goes past on top of the viaduct and during the day I can't see the train. During the summer when the trees are all dressed the train disappears behind their leaves. The full majesty of the train comes into its own at night when it's dark with its caterpillar body studded with diamonds, rubies and amber as it flashes past like a shiny bracelet and I think *I must buy one before I leave here*. I haven't – yet.

***

For a time I read everything on palmistry. I'm really interested in palms. Mine are deeply lined in thick strokes, very clear, and you can tell which line is which. They're not busy like my friend Manda's are. My friend Manda never stops talking. It's like she has some sort of verbal diarrhoea. I notice the palms of her hands are seriously lined, there's hardly a blank space on them, and I wonder if this means she can't stop talking. Thumbs are also interesting. My thumb is straight and has very little bend in it (not to mention very little skin!), which used to upset me because I'd heard that thumbs that don't bend backwards mean you are not generous and I always thought I was a very generous soul. Nevertheless, I've since learnt that if you have a major bend it means you're kind of weak, generous but weak. Everyone at school wanted to have double-jointed thumbs, thumbs that you could pull down to touch your wrist. I could never do that but I can manipulate my mouth into a zig-zag, lifting one side up one way and the other down to the opposite side and I can fold my tongue bringing the edges up to the middle. I can't touch the tip of my nose with my tongue though. I can imagine you all pulling horrendous faces and pushing thumbs back as you read this!

***

I've just been on a mindfulness course because I intend to be even more mindful. It was a six-week course and we all met up in a village hall on a Wednesday evening from 6.00 to 8.45pm. We sat on chairs and helped ourselves to a raisin, which we were required to hold in the palm of our hand and study in depth. Naturally enough, my raisin fell on the floor, which was embarrassing. The carpeted floor wasn't that clean but I hastily picked it up. Then we had to put it in our mouth and feel its texture on our tongue (did I have to?) but I did. It was all to do with slowing down and taking time to notice and I really enjoyed that.

***

Do you think you die when you stop wanting to learn or being inquisitive or when you've lost interest in living life? Is that why people get dementia because they no longer wish to participate in living? Perhaps their partner is controlling – not in a nasty way although perhaps they are but in the way of being helpful: 'Don't worry, darling, I'll do that. No, no; you go and lie down and rest and I'll do that for you'.

***

Then there are the wives who haven't a clue where anything is when their partner/husband dies. They've no idea where the cheque book is, where the bank statements are, where the investments and savings are. All their married lives, these wives have allowed their husbands complete autonomous control, the wives probably being given a little pocket money or housekeeping. 'You go off and buy a little something to cheer yourself up with'. That's all acceptable. Really? I think my parents did that because when my mother died she only had £900 in her bank account. She did have some beautiful jewellery though, which was what my father had bought her over the years.

***

I do all the right meditation things. I've even got an app on my phone and, once I close my eyes whilst sitting bolt (no, gently) upright, with my hands cupped upward (to let the good energy come in), I take my vision inward. Off I go... *calm, calm; breathe in, breathe out, breathe in, breathe out. Just wondering what to cook today; God, remember that time you left the saucepan on the gas? Thank goodness the gas was on really low... Come back to your breathing; calm, calm; breathe in...* If I'm sitting on a chair to meditate, I must remember to uncross my legs and plant my feet firmly on the floor because someone once told me that otherwise the energy doesn't know where to go. Why that should make a difference? I have no idea as, after all, a lot of people sit cross-legged on the floor to meditate.

I'm middle-aged now – well, more than, actually – and wondering whether I'm enlightened. I've just been listening to Melvyn Bragg and his *In Our Time* podcast and today on my Tolly walk it was all about Zen. I bloody well should be, frankly; after all, over all these years I am doing everything – I meditate every day and I practise yoga. I notice now that when I'm in Downward Dog, for instance, my arms have gone all crinkly and old-looking and when I'm in plank I can't look back and see my feet, my boobs get in the way. I once had a yoga teacher who always commented on my colourful toes, as she called them. Sometimes the toes were red or purple and it didn't worry me as such then but these days if my toes turn a nasty shade of red, or worse, I worry. It's happening on the backs of my hands too, the crinkly bit, I mean.

I come across all sorts of things on my Tolly walks. There's a graveyard of tree trunks, which look to me like a mass of skeletons. I have my whale that I pat and say hello to and to the left of her I imagine it's her baby. I try to squeeze myself into the hollowed out tree, but I'm not as thin as I used to be so I content myself by just giving her a brief squeeze. Later there's a really long piece of wood buried in the pathway and I imagine it's a Viking ship even though we are at least eight miles from the sea.

***

Even now, many years later, I still get that sinking heart feeling whenever Jerome's name comes up.

***

On a lighter note, I saw my friend Lizanne earlier. I'd made soup for her, brought her a roast chicken and, at 87 years old, she remains a hugely glamorous-looking woman. She now relives her younger years and how she had 22 proposals of marriage in her lifetime, something she is immensely proud of. With a cheeky glint in her eye, she reminisces about her glory years, which are alive in her imagination. With her large rotund body and very swollen, sore legs, I am agog but go along with her fantasy because why in heck not?

In all my reading – and I've read a lot – the one thing that always comes up is gratitude. In interviews with celebrities or the very rich or both, they are always very grateful and appreciative. I begin to think that maybe there's something in that. Maybe if I showed more gratitude in my life, being thankful for a simple act of kindness perhaps or just feeling grateful, my life might improve. That's why I have my gratitude list.

Chapter Thirty-Eight

Friendship

I feel on the edge of my friendship group nowadays. I definitely don't want to go back to those friends I had before, many of them dispersed now in either alcoholic gloom or should that be doom? This being on the edge of things like friendships makes me feel sad and in the next breath or thought, I think I'm being too sensitive and doing my usual overthinking of stuff. With Facebook now, I have a couple of unthinking 'friends' who like to tag other friends about getting together or how lovely it was to be together at the weekend and I'm thinking: *Hello? Why wasn't I invited or included? I was excluded so obviously, so why did that something have to be aired?* On the edge, that's me.

I definitely don't want any friends who are not 100 per cent behind me, which is why I have had to let some friendships go and keep others at arm's length. When I was in my bad place, there were half a dozen good friends who were there for me through thick and thin. I don't think anyone rooted for me, though; no-one solidly behind me. A lot of friends wouldn't take sides, which was kind of shocking and I definitely think that, as women we must support each other in all ways, and most definitely in times of trouble.

Perhaps it's a case of getting older and friends moving away or just moving on or they don't move on at all. I went to a 50th birthday party a while ago, not really wanting to be there, but Julia's one of those old friends and I felt I ought to (it's that bloody school motto that keeps coming back to annoy me – 'ought' and 'should'). When I arrive, I am swept back to the 70s. A few of the guests have their lank, greasy, grey hair, flowing robes and are smoking bongs, for crying out loud, and saying, 'Yeah, man', with missing teeth and legs wobbling backwards.

***

I have tried and tried to help Jax but nothing I do or say seems to get through to her. Perhaps I am spouting too much 'spiritual' stuff but whatever I try to advise, she just won't have it and says I'm too interfering: 'Just shut up, Penskew'. For instance, she's always complaining about her work so I suggest that perhaps she could do something else:

"You're really good with dogs and cats, Jax, and already you look after some of your neighbours' pets when they're away. Why don't you set up a dog walking business or a pet sitting service? You'd be really good at that. I'll get some leaflets printed and we can drop them through letterboxes and stick them on lamp-posts," but it comes to nothing.

Her life has become one large frazzle, which might also have something to do with the unending heat of south Florida. The thing is is that I feel as if I've lost my best friend. I'm hoping this is temporary. It seems to me she lives on the surface of life and that there's nothing more to think about apart from getting through a day. I don't know how to help her and I think that's the bottom line – you can't help someone if they don't want to be helped and, of course, she doesn't think she needs help. There's something missing within her. She never does what she says she's going to do and thinks that there's nothing she can do to change anything. She also tries to fit in too much in her day (which is unchanged) and why she's still always late. All this time and I keep bloody well forgiving you. We have so much history, you and I; but you like everyone, even those who do not deserve your like. Jax can be a really good friend and will always be happy to help when she can, although not necessarily in the time you would like.

It came to me that summer you were home – not home for you anymore – home for me is England and Sussex. I'd just left the husband and myself and the girls of six and 15 were living in our small terraced cottage. Small the house may have been, but I was becoming myself again after all those years of turmoil, having lost myself.

We hadn't managed to spend a lot of time together, not as much as usual because you were staying with your sister, and of course she always has a timetable for you to adhere to. Well, on this particular summer's evening we sat in the garden for a catch-up and a glass of chilled white wine. You did look lovely, all nicely made up wearing a floaty chiffon top I seem to remember, and I said:

"You didn't have to dress up for me, Jax, but how nice that you'd made the effort." Then, after a second glass of wine, you said:

"Well, must be off; going round to Jerome's..."

I was floored. "Why?"

"He may be your ex-husband, but I like him."

Uh-oh, there she goes all flouncy and floaty and I feel bereft and, *how dare she?* Worst of all is that Jerome couldn't care less about Jax and I dread the combination of her having too much to drink and his charm.

These days, it comes as a surprise when I find there are people – friends, my children – who actually *do* love me and tell me that they do. I realise that I have three choices that will lead me to greater freedom and authenticity: 1. Not worrying about what people think. 2. Not being bound by convention or how I was raised, and 3. Not thinking about what I ought to be doing, just knowing that I try to always do the right thing.

Chapter Thirty-Nine

2016

It's my 60th birthday, which was such hard work to organise by myself. Thank goodness I have money so I can pay for it to be catered for and don't have that hassle. I've arranged for a marquee and invited 75 people. My home is looking stunning with its huge views over the fields. I've hired tables and chairs, outside lights and, actually, I'm dead excited in the run up to the event. The day itself arrives and the weather is – frankly – crap, cold, drizzly, wet and windy but, after all, it *is* February and I'm not downhearted. *Who cares about a bit of cold and wet?* The fire pit is lit, sort of; it keeps blowing out and then suddenly all the electrics go out. *Oh flip, now what?* Luckily, the guys who have set up the marquee and outside lights have a generator and they've worked out that the electrics in my house can't cope with all the extra electricity outside, so they swap stuff around and eventually the electrics come back on and we are on for a partaaayy.

My children have created a playlist of music – I wouldn't know where to start with all that – and I've asked guests not to bring gifts, got too much stuff already. I asked them to please bring their drinks; instead they bring a flower shop. I have SO many flowers that I haven't got enough containers for them all and why couldn't they bloody well bring a bottle? Actually, there are bottles a-plenty but I feel really detached. Maybe it's the lousy weather or the fact that there are certain people that simply don't care about other people's property as, when it came to clearing up, I found food had been smashed into the carpet and, bearing in mind it was curry we were all eating, I couldn't get the stains out.

You know what? I remember looking out at the mass of people and thinking *I won't do this again*, even though I love a party. I just don't think I can be bothered, especially when I've had many parties over the years and invited so-called good friends over for supper, for drinks, for a simple evening gathering, and do I get an invite back? Hardly.

**

Come the summer my plum tree is laden with plums and I've decided to have a small summer soiree with just a few friends. It's a lovely sunny day and I say to my friend, Sue, that I couldn't possibly eat or use all the plums and knowing her husband loves to make his own alcoholic drinks, I suggested they might like to collect a few. And they did – completely stripping my tree of every single plum; nothing was left and when I asked about the plums and whether they had managed to use them all? Oh yes, and you'd think they would have offered me a bottle, but all had been drunk.

Chapter Forty

Volunteering

I've begun volunteering at my local hospice and I am privileged to be able to do this and to at last give back. The hospice is mainly for the terminally ill cancer patients but there are also patients with the diseases of motor neurone and multiple sclerosis. There is a café, which is open Tuesdays, Thursdays and Fridays and on these days patients come in for various treatments like reflexology or reiki, others for counselling. Creative writing courses are available as well as art therapy and all-sorts and I love it. I am absolutely amazed because I come across all these incredible people.

On Mondays I'm in the café from 10–2, which is where I serve coffee and food to visitors who are seeing patients on the ward and staff can order a meal. Thursdays I'm on the floor with the outpatients 1–4. I've also become a befriender, which means that I go and visit a terminally ill patient in their home. I've been allocated Don. He's in his 80s and lives on his own in a bungalow as his wife died a couple of years ago. I'm not sure what he's ill with precisely but mainly he's lonely so I visit every Wednesday. He's obviously been a very practical man in his day, an electrician, and is now frustrated that he can't do all the things that he was used to doing when he was fit and healthy.

Why he decided to go on the roof to paint the bloody chimney is beyond me. It took two ladders, one to get to the flat roof and the second to be put up against the chimney stack, but having got to the flat roof he fell over and lay there for possibly hours before a neighbour saw him and it took a fire engine and a crane to hoist him off and over the roof to be dumped gently in his front garden. An ambulance awaited him. Then, blow me, he tries to do the same thing again the following week and now he's in hospital.

It's been a couple of weeks since I've seen him, so I ring the hospital to ask if Don would like me to visit. He would and I do. In the meantime, all hell has broken loose at the hospice because I didn't inform them of my intended hospital visit and I am in deep trouble. I get a two-page letter using words like 'boundaries', 'self-importance' and 'martyrdom' and it has really upset me. When I show the letter to my manager she is aghast, too, and bravely tries to fight my corner, but it's no good. Rules have been broken and I am not in favour. I try really hard to get over this but I've lost respect and when sorry isn't forthcoming, I decide enough is enough and I leave.

So much for giving back, eh? I did love the hospice though, so I am sad about that.

Chapter Forty-One

Rome and Rant

I'm not sure if it's because I'm reading Sigrid Rausing's *Mayhem: a memoir*, but I've suddenly become horrible and impatient with a nasty turn of phrase. Not that I'm blaming Ms Rausing for this, not at all. I've just returned from a long weekend in Rome – my maiden name and, after all, I'm in my 60th year and I've never visited before, so myself and the youngest go. In my going to Rome I realise I am not a cheap tourist, I like to travel in 5* luxury and so we stay at a 5* hotel, a really swanky one, but surfaces can be deceptive. The sumptuous infinity pool on the roof looked huge in the photos but in fact is rather small. If more than three people get in, it would be a little crowded. To get into the pool itself, one has to walk in the boiling sun across the decking, burning the soles of your feet in the process. Nevertheless, I have become this crosspatchy person all in the last few days (please don't let me become like Gaga or my mother for that matter). At my vast age I have decided I won't put up with inefficiency or nonsense anymore. I think it's because I'm a single woman.

It was our last full day and we decided to just lounge by the pool when I espied a delicious-looking sandwich platter held aloft coming by and being delivered graciously to a couple on the other side of the pool. It looked scrummy, so I asked the server if I could have that exact same plate of food. 'No problem, Madam'. A short while later my sandwich duly arrived and looked nothing like the sumptuous offering I'd seen walk by. The server dutifully explained that unfortunately they had run out of French fries and was I okay to have these crisps instead.

"Err, no," I replied. "How is it possible that a 5* establishment can run out of potatoes?"

The sandwich itself consisted of just a tiny layer of tuna with raw onion, smothered in mayonnaise. On checking the menu, I see that my 'sandwich' was supposed to be a club and come with not only French fries but pomodoro, too, all for the princely sum of €15. I complain and get my money back. I don't understand why people can't do their jobs properly and try to get away with crap.

Chapter Forty-Two

Tolly

In another house I lived in, I could take Tolly for her 'walkies' up a narrow footpath and up towards Lodge Hill. I did this occasionally but found I got a little claustrophobic walking that way as it's all hemmed in with fences and 'Beware of the cows', 'Do not let your dog off the leash' or 'Sheep about' notices.

I much prefer going to the common where there is a huge pond that, up until last year, had two beautiful swans living on it. There's a hideaway island in the middle with lots of trees and bushes for ducks to hide in. Overall, it's a huge open space with different paths to walk on. The trouble is it hasn't stopped raining this last month of March and walkies is almost impossible; it's more like slurping, slipping and sinking. I can't guarantee I can do an hour of actual walking because it's taking so flippin' long to navigate through the mud. The swans are a little scary and have this habit of stealthily gliding along, pretending to take no notice of my Tolly girl splashing in the water after her ball, and then suddenly there's an enormous crashing sound as they flap their vast wings at full pelt and are on the attack of my girl. I scream and shout and start to undress ready to jump in; I don't care who's about. Tolly doesn't give two hoots about them; she only wants her bloody ball. Then one day they were no longer there. The last I heard, the female swan had swallowed a fish hook and died and the male was shot with an air pistol. I've been walking here for at least three years and I've watched them become parents and what good parents they are, but every year their babies are either taken or they die, they never grow to full size. It makes me sad and mad. I don't understand why the council allow the pond to be fished all year round for fishermen to catch the same old fish day in, day out. In very dry weather when the water level has gone down, fishermen still fish. Where is the pleasure in that?

Tolly is ball-obsessed, which is something I don't remember training her for, although I do remember thinking when she was a puppy that I hoped she would love to run and fetch a ball. I've also become ball-obsessed and will search out balls in the bushes, in the tall grass and I jump around excitedly when I find one, which I secrete away to replace the ones that she loses. I have about 30 tennis balls in the boot of my car! Lately, she's got a new ball obsession which is to drop her ball, usually somewhere that I can't reach or even see, and then she dashes off to hide behind a tree trunk, so I can't find her either. This is a huge waste of time. I'm wondering if this is something she's copied from when I used to hide from her and, even now, I giggle at the memory of our hiding games. I used to play hide and seek with Ringo and Loppy too, our black labs in Assam.

I think about my Tolly girl who came to us when she was so little but instinctively knew how to clean herself. When she was little and still pooing and weeing she used to sleep on the kitchen lino floor, safe, and at around 4am her little whimpers would start. I had that same connection with her as I had with my own children when they were babies. I am instantly awake at her slightest cry and so I creep downstairs. She and I will snuggle under a blanket on the sofa in the sitting room and fall back to sleep until it is a sensible time to wake up. At that time it was 7am. Tolly has taught me patience.

I know people who are nuts about their pets but I'm not one of them. I am not a natural pet owner, just as I'm not one of those earth mothers. Although I absolutely adore Tolly, I look upon it as a job and a responsibility. I think I was like this with my oldest child. I can't just walk out and go off for a few hours leaving her at home on her own, so in that way it is just like having a toddler. I know people who find it hard to go on holiday for two weeks because they miss their cats SO much. It took years before I became more spontaneous whereas otherwise it was routine. I'd get cross, for instance, if Manda called at 7pm, which was the exact time I would be putting H to bed when she was an only child. We've done a swap now, Manda and I – I'm all for spontaneity but she can't do anything without it being arranged weeks in advance.

***

It's early summer where I live now and I notice the birds are really noisy late into the evening, still chattering away at 9pm. I imagine them having lovely conversations, telling each other what they've done that day. On my Tolly walks there are lots of ducks and quite often a female is surrounded by many males, which I find a little disconcerting because the males are quite aggressive and I notice they peck at the one and only female, almost drowning her. When I look this up, I am horrified to read that female ducks are regularly raped by the males, it's like they're part of a harem where male ducks get their way whenever they like. Bloody hell.

Living in this supposed idyll, however, I am surrounded by 'snotsville'. These are the people who drive enormous 4x4 cars, usually very big black ones with tinted rear windows so their little darlings can't be spied upon, which take up the whole of the narrow high street. These cars are immaculately clean; there isn't a speck of anything on them. All they care about is making sure they are seen to be driving expensive brand new cars with their designer sunglasses and designer kids. Whoopee-doo. It's funny because, to my way of thinking, they want to stand out with their shiny cars with darkened windows, toned bodies and tied back hair but they end up all looking exactly like each other. No different then to how my parents' generation were with their fear of not doing the right thing – their 'one mustn't be different' or rock the boat attitude.

It's early March and my window looks out to a field where sheep are grazing and baby lambs are skittering about. My study window is covered with brown ivy, which has yet to come into new leaf and I just feel so damn happy. I've only recently moved to this cottage that's hidden away around the back of the high street and the joy is that I can walk to the shops, walk to a pub – walk – without having to get in my car. I've never enjoyed that before, having always lived pretty rurally that you couldn't get anywhere, like a shop for instance, unless you drove. Mind you, I will only walk to the shops if it's a 5-minute walk away, otherwise I drive – I'm always in a rush, see.

I am mesmerised by the sheep over the road and can spend long minutes just watching and then of course I get a feeling of guilt because I feel I 'should/ought' to be doing something other than watching the sheep and feeling happy just doing that. I also feel sad that those young baby lambs will only live a few months before being killed and I start to think about becoming vegetarian.

In my current life everything has become simpler and I don't care what anybody says, having money is hugely helpful. I loved the times when I didn't have enough and when I look at the celebrity world I wonder how they are in their palatial houses with umpteen bedrooms and more bathrooms that you can possibly use sensibly. What's the point? No, just give me my small 3-bedroom house where every room is in regular use; I am happy with that. When you have so much money and you've got to the top of whatever pedestal you are on, where do you go from there? When do you say 'enough is enough'? That's what I say to myself.

I have a lawn mowing man at my present house. I'd like to call him a gardener but as he says 'You ain't got a garden, love, it's more of a field', I don't feel I can! He's right; I do have dandelions and all sorts coming up amongst the blades of grass. Anyway, he's coming here on Friday because he wants to get the grass down to a '4', whatever that means. I'm looking for stripes in a lawn but I don't think I'll be able to have that.

The other thing is that I've done very well after all these long years dealing with everything on my own, so I need to acknowledge myself here.

Chapter Forty-Three

Cooking in my house

As you may remember from my earlier years, I said I wasn't very good at cooking. I'm still not very good at cooking when I'm on my own here in the house; I'm on my own now because the youngest has gone off travelling for three months. I started to drink kefir because I read in a magazine that this celebrity nutritionist recommends it to everyone. She drinks it herself so I went to try to find some. Goodness, it took ages – nothing on-line, which would have been the simplest way to get hold of it. In the end I found some in an actual shop on the high street and I've been slurping the stuff ever since. I'm hoping it's going to settle my stomach because I do have a tendency to get an upset tummy perhaps once a week, sometimes more. I put it down to drinking milk and having butter for breakfast – lashings of butter, which I slather thickly onto warm toast with a sprinkling of sugar–that always seem to upset it, but since I've been on this kefir, I think it's helping. I juiced, too, today; it's beetroot, spinach, apple, celery stalk, and three small satsumas and that helps too. Best of all for me is the sliced raw ginger in hot water first thing every morning.

When I unload the dishwasher I restack plates and bowls under the ones that are already stored in the cupboard so that each item gets used in turn and I don't use the same plate twice in succession. I don't like leaving plates or anything out on their own (and ensure that Jax isn't in the vicinity!) I need to make sure that every plate or bowl has a turn at being utilised. It's like my lonesome tooth at the back of my mouth –I've lost the one beside it to an abscess and it now has no other tooth to talk to.

So while I am slightly obsessed with the arrangement of my plates and bowls, my best friend in the whole wide world is colour-coordinating her hangers!

Chapter Forty-Four

Getting older

How old do you have to be before you are considered old? For me, it's when things start dropping off and I start tripping over my stomach fat or, more likely, my boobs. I am very happy in my own company; I don't need to talk to other people although it is a shame when something funny happens on the TV and I'm laughing all on my own, but I'd rather be like this on my own than in a lousy, lonely relationship. I've just realised that since I left Jerome, no man has asked me out. God! Well, it just shows how little I've missed that.

For the first time in my fairly long life so far, I have absolutely nothing I have to do. I don't have an office to go to, I don't have any freelance secretarial work coming to me, I've given up my stall at the Vintage and Antiques market, no reflexology work and no soup making; I'm not beholden to anyone and I am pretty much free to do exactly as I please. Of course, I do still need to take my Tolly girl for her walkies twice a day. The current situation is hugely pleasurable but tinged with a little bit of guilt because my head says 'You really should be doing something – you can't sit around reading, you know'.

I have found some sort of contentment with my life and have decided that I am going to relax into my future. I'm not going to spend whatever time I have left of my life feeling guilty or useless or being busy and stressed and nobody is going to put me down ever again. I am stopping all that.

I don't keep my emotions in; it's not a good idea. Write everything down if you can; just do it. Be more like a zebra from that book by Robert M Sapolsky on *Why Zebras Don't get Ulcers* – except, of course, it isn't so easy when you're amongst stress on a constant basis.

The oldest has already left home to live a good independent life in London and my youngest is off travelling and will leave soon too, quite rightly. Then what happens? What happens to me? Do I just continue to age because it is already happening rather rapidly? Goodness, when I look around I see many women my age who behave as though they are already almost dead. *Please God, not me*, is what I say to Him whenever I come across these ashen-faced undeads as I call them. The question here is: why? Why do women of 55+ years want to look like their mothers did? Is it so biologically ingrained in their history that this is how it is supposed to be? I remember a good friend of mine, many, many years ago when I was approaching 40, saying to me (I had long hair then, still do):

"Well, you'll have to cut your hair short, you know."

"Why?"

"Well, it'll be ridiculous at your age to still have long hair."

Oh, right. Well, she *is* my age and looks ancient, poor thing. The thing is, maybe I do look old but perhaps one can't see oneself if you see what I mean and perhaps that's what it's all about. Perhaps there is a secret grand scheme whereby everyone around you who is your age looks older than you – because you are you and you've known yourself all your life, you think you look the same.

In the village where I used to live there are an awful lot of undeads with their grey lank hair, lack of make-up, no lipstick, and every one of these so-called undeads looks deeply unhappy with their lot and I feel sad for them. I would love to go up to them, give them a big hug and say 'Come on, here we all have one life, live it well'. I don't, of course, and they will continue with what, to them, is a life of sorts. I know quite a few myself who are quite content enough not to stretch themselves out too much, not living a BIG LIFE. Happy with mediocrity, that's not me.

In my younger days I wore stockings and sometimes forgot to wear knickers, but today I don't look like Jacqueline Bisset anymore. Someone once said I did a long, long time ago. Instead, I am joyful today.

There comes a point in an evening when I go into automatic pilot mode and basically switch off. It's usually at 9pm. I have little tricks to remind me that, for instance, I have brushed my teeth. I leave the toothbrush on the basin rather than putting it back in the glass.

I'm in bed by 10pm and write down anything that I need to

remember for the following day – maybe P has asked me to wake her at 9am, things like that because it is bloody annoying when I don't remember stuff and that happens quite a lot these days and takes me back to those awful times when I drank to excess – and forgot. Also, I write down my gratitudes: 'Thank you for my great, good life, thank you. Thank you for my HEALTH, wealth, goodness, kindness and LOVE, thank you. Thank you for the strength of my body and of my mind.' These days I add in 'What is my purpose?' but I'm not getting any answers to that.

Chapter Fourty-Five

Joy and Patterns

I am joyful every day and sometimes I worry that I am far too happy and content and any minute all this joy I feel will come crashing down, but it's been years now and it hasn't, not yet. Maybe that's why I keep seeing kisses in the sky and matching numbers on clocks like 16.16 or 06.06.

Woke up this morning at 06.06 – oh good, okay – everything will go smoothly today.

What I don't want and what I would like

I'm going to make a list of all the things I don't want to do anymore:

- I don't want to have mundane conversations and I couldn't care less what you're wearing.
- I don't want to walk for the sake of walking. I love to walk my dog but there's got to be a reason to walk. However, I do think that when my Tolly girl is no more, I must keep up some sort of walking, it would be so easy just to laze about.
- I don't want to join a choir or be in a group like a book club.
- I don't want to go out for dinner late in the evening. I prefer to either go out early evening, say 6pm for drinks, and I much prefer a late lunch and then not to eat again for the rest of the day.
- I don't want to make any new friends. I've got my handful and that's fine.
- I don't want to watch explicit sex on television.
- I don't want to watch terrible violence either, especially if it concerns animals.

- I don't want to ride a bike after that time I forgot to turn the handlebar and crashed straight into the wall of my neighbour's house.
- I definitely don't want to go on a cruise. I think cruising is for very old people in their 70s and 80s.

The things I still want to do

- I want to still be involved in my children's lives but allow them space:
- I want to write this book.
- I want to continue to write daily.
- I want to always be curious.

Goodness, this is a very short list...

Chapter Forty-Six

Being

I'm not prepared to live a mediocre life even though I spend most of my days on my own. I think the thing with me is that I am hugely sensitive and emotional. My now ex-husband has dropped off three boxes of old photos that include lots of my oldest in her toddler days but when I get to the second box I notice there are many of Jane. Here's one of her sunbathing and it's a close-up of her sunbathing face and cleavage; another of her looking directly at the camera with a sultry smile on her face. It's got me thinking – were Jerome and Jane in a relationship when we'd just got married? When I Messenger Jane's ex-husband to ask, he confirms that we were conned, our marriages were lies right from the start, which you may remember is what I touched on earlier. Blimey, I suddenly feel like Princess Diana when she said there were three people in her marriage and I feel terribly sad.

In 2018, I found a letter I had written to my mother after she died. I'd written it a couple of years after I left Jerome:

'My darling Mummy. I love you so much and I miss you. I wish you could be here to see my children – H soooo great and I think since I've told her about me and Jerome a whole weight has lifted off her. I wish you could be here because Daddy's not – although he's here in different ways. Are you helping me? Please can you let me know if you are there? What will you show me? Perhaps a bird? I love you. Penny xxxxxx'

...and the carriage clock that hasn't worked in forever started ticking.

***

When I found that letter, I felt tearful and realised that no-one is equipped for the job of parenting. We can only do our best based on the experiences we've had in our own childhoods. Everyone is just doing the best they can.

***

I think I can now be classed as a grown-up. I've got a wild flower garden going on and I am even growing tomatoes in a pot. I thought you had to be old to enjoy gardening. *Oh...* I am fast forwarding to old quicker than I like and I don't like gardening anyway.

I am beginning to think about death and I must start getting organised about it. Do I need to buy a plot? Shall I pay in advance for my funeral? I don't want my girls to be concerned with paying out. What about a coffin and what type? I think I'll go for a wicker one and there's a natural burial ground near here so maybe I'll go and check it out. Do I want to be buried or cremated? All these questions. The thing is, my mother's side of the family were not long-lived and that's a little scary although there is that fifty-fifty chance for me as my father's side did a lot better age-wise.

I wonder who will greet me when I die. I do hope none of my dead relatives turn up.

***

I will not get frumpy. I dye my hair and grow it long. Okay, I am not particularly happy with my toilet-S-bend-shaped body but I'm healthy, eat healthily and I have a routine. I like to think that I am always curious about the world; that I am constantly wishing to learn as much as possible. I try very hard to do the best I can especially where my children are concerned. Just recently though, I'm beginning to question whether being this kind of thoughtful and being brave are actually good enough. What if my thinking of myself as being good is actually not? What if I do all this 'good' stuff, think good thoughts, eat good food, be kind but then, God forbid, get into an accident and die or become paralysed or something awful like that? Does that only happen in fiction stories or murder mysteries on TV?

Honestly, for the first time at this time of my life, this is joy. Instead of feeling guilty and thinking, *OMG, what am I going to do for the rest of my life? What am I going to do all day every day?* I feel as if I am allowed to *be*, that I have actually gained something from all the counselling I've had, the books I've read, the mindfulness courses I've been on, the meditation and yoga stuff that I regularly do and the so-called 'spiritual' journeys (all of them!) I've been going on for all this time. It's exhausting when I think back, so I'm bloody well going to enjoy myself albeit in a thoughtful way. I am in gurgling happiness.

What I am is centred. I am as fully aware as I can be and fully present and I don't think about the future or look for a worry to worry about. Thank goodness for my diaries of which I have many, many volumes going right back to when my oldest was two years old – that's because there's a lot in my past that I've forgotten about or perhaps that's what happens as you get older and you can only remember the seriously major events. I do think that I've lost a certain enthusiasm for things, like package holidays for instance, oh, and reading a newspaper, and I've definitely lost that desire to buy stuff, clothes, etc. I do not need to buy anything more. There are some people I know who spend days shopping and will spend a small fortune in the purchase of that particular handbag of which they already have eight or nine or they'll spend days, even weeks, before their holiday getting ready – laying their clothes out on the bed, buying new clothes to take and packing way before they need to.

As I said, I've got to a time in my life where I don't need to buy anything anymore. I've got enough clothes and shoes. There's nothing out there that I want. Obviously, on occasions, I do have to replace things like socks and knickers and bras, but otherwise – no.

Life has been a bit of a struggle really and it is only now as I look back that I see how far I have come. I wonder, too, what it is that makes me begin this process of looking back. I'm not sick – please no, thank goodness, but it is a fact that when people become sick or something shocking happens to them, they begin to assess their lives and perhaps assess what went wrong in order to start to put it right or they begin to appreciate the everyday. I found this out when I did my hospice volunteering and how remarkable these terminally ill cancer patients were now that they'd had such a terrible diagnosis.

Nevertheless, I don't want to get sick first in order to feel alive, so I'm trying to make sure I bloody well live in the moment every single day and know that I am alive.

I am feeling very grateful. I am so able to do a lot of good in the world but perhaps I'll just stick to my own little world right here for now. I have a most fantastic relationship with my children; they are the blessings of my heart and I treasure them.

It isn't easy to *be* and to be present and to want good things to happen to you after all the crap. I love my life right now, this minute – this is it. *I am.*

In silence you come to me
In silence you become aware
In silence you have your reason
In silence you have a prayer
In this quiet moment of time
When nothing is all I hear
I would love to find your mind
And simply float you there
When all is said and done
Yet nothing has been said
Let's look inside ourselves
And trust in what we create
Peace comes from knowing
The very soul of you
And happiness becomes your master
So thank the lord for YOU.

THE END

Printed in Great Britain
by Amazon

24611373R00126